Harris Ray Greene

The English Language

Its grammatical and logical principles

Harris Ray Greene

The English Language
Its grammatical and logical principles

ISBN/EAN: 9783337085360

Printed in Europe, USA, Canada, Australia, Japan

Cover: Foto ©Paul-Georg Meister /pixelio.de

More available books at **www.hansebooks.com**

THE
SPANISH TEACHER

AND

Colloquial Phrase-Book:

AN EASY AND AGREEABLE METHOD

OF ACQUIRING A

SPEAKING KNOWLEDGE

OF THE

SPANISH LANGUAGE.

TWELFTH EDITION.
Revised & Corrected.

By **FRANCIS BUTLER**,

TEACHER AND TRANSLATOR OF LANGUAGES.

NEW YORK:
D. APPLETON AND COMPANY,
1, 3, AND 5 BOND STREET.
1881.

PREFACE.

All nations have been, and continue to be, abundantly supplied with *new* methods of acquiring foreign languages; but, has any one of these theories succeeded to any extent in producing that *speaking knowledge* which is the first essential to mutual communication?

Tongue and language *were* synonymous, but the interpretation thereof has been wofully perverted; since, among the *thousands* in this great city who have studied a foreign *language*, how many may there be capable of common conversation in the *tongue* which they considered as a necessary appendage to a polite or commercial education? Alas! how few!

The author of this little work aims at nothing new; has no magical method of imparting a whole language for 25 cents; has no new theory to advance;—but wishes herein simply to demonstrate, that if *a little child can learn to speak a language without difficulty,* much more easily may the same instinct matured by reason and experience, obtain the same knowledge, in the same old-fashioned way. Try it; you cannot fail of success.

New York, July 4th, **1849.**

CONTENTS.

	Page.
Advice to the Student,	5
Pronunciation of the Spanish Alphabet,	11
Remarks,	16
Articles and Nouns in common use,	17
Verbs arranged alphabetically,	21
Adjectives in common use,	25
Personal Pronouns,	27
Possessive Pronouns,	28
Adverbs, etc.,	29
Interjections.	33
The days of the week, and the months.	34
The Numbers,	34
To have, affirmatively, followed by an object,	39
To have, negatively,	41
To have, interrogatively,	42
To have, negatively and interrogatively,	43
To be, affirmatively,	44
To be, negatively.	47
To be, interrogatively,	49
To be, negatively and interrogatively,	50
Titles,	52
To ask questions,	52
To salute and inquire after the health of some person,	56
Getting up.	59
To dress one's self,	60
Asking and thanking,	63
To consult,	65
To affirm and deny.	67
Going to school,	70
On the Spanish language,	78
Of the seasons,	80
Of the weather,	82
Of epochs,	85
Of the hour,	88
News,	90
Of the age,	93
Morning,	94
Of the necessaries of life,	96
Of the fire,	97
Going to market,	99
Breakfast,	101
Dinner,	103
Tea,	106
Supper,	107
Going to bed,	108
Inquiries relative to a journey,	111
Parting,	113
Inquiring one's way,	114
Inquiring for the residence of a person.	116
Meeting a friend,	117
Going and coming,	118
The walk,	123
Walk in a garden,	124
Evening,	128
To write a letter,	129
Needle-work,	131
A visit,	132
Drawing,	133
At an exhibition of paintings,	135
Expressions of surprise.	138
Expressions of probability,	139
Expressions of joy,	140
Expressions of sorrow,	141
Expressions of blame,	142
Expressions of anger.	143
Expressions of antipathy,	145
Expressions of sympathy,	146
With the tailor,	147
At a woollen-draper's,	151
At a linen-draper's,	152
At a perfumer's,	154
At a bookseller's,	156
At a jeweller's,	159
At a watchmaker's.	162
To engage a man-servant,	164
To engage a female servant,	166
At a shoemaker's.	168
With a dressmaker,	169
To play at chess,	171
Collection of detached sentences,	173
CONJUGATION OF VERBS.	
Estar and Ser,	269
Remarks on Estar and Ser,	272
Haber and Tener,	273
Remarks on Haber and Tener,	275
Amar, regular verb of the First Conjugation,	276
Irregular verbs of the first conjugation,	278
Temer, regular verb of the Second Conjugation,	281
Irregular verbs of the second conjugation,	283
Sufrir, regular verb of the Third Conjugation.	287
Irregular verbs of the third conjugation.	290

ADVICE TO THE STUDENT,

ON THE

METHOD OF STUDYING A FOREIGN LANGUAGE.

To acquire a speaking knowledge of a foreign language is not a difficult task, if undertaken in a good humor, and with a fixed determination to make some little progress every day. There are so many little bits of time, which, if devoted to study, would tend rather to relieve than annoy. The time that is disagreeably wasted in waiting for others, for boats, stages, breakfast, dinner, tea, supper, etc., might be both profitably and pleasureably wiled away, by taking a small and interesting book from the coat pocket. Beside this, there is the advantage of oftentimes meeting with those to whom you may refer in case of difficulty. The writer has learned more of foreign languages in this way, than he could have acquired in closeted hours of deep and wearisome toil and study. "Many mickles make a muckle," says the Scotchman; so say I; and so you will find, if you will follow the simple course laid down for you.

To speak a language, you must begin precisely as a child begins to speak its mother tongue. A child has never been known to speak his first sentences correctly, but acquires his knowledge of language in the same way as he learns to run. He begins by jumping and springing in his mother's arms, then crawls, then toddles, cautious but resolute, from chair to chair, till after a few self-taught lessons in experimental philosophy, he can scamper, unguided and alone. So it is with his pronouncing organs; he begins with mum, mum, and goes on exercising his tongue, etc., soon adopting a method of his own of regulating his accents to the sounds of others. But I never knew a child stop speaking, because he was afraid of making a mistake; if such were the case, this would indeed be a silent world. Don't be afraid; you will soon be amused at the blunders you *have* made, and your constant progress will impart to you fresh courage. You will acquire a talkative knowledge of a language, by the same means as the child.

The majority of those who study a foreign language seldom dream of making any use of it; they dread the bare idea of speaking a word, but appear to be perfectly satisfied with having taken so many quarter's lessons, translated from such and such books, and, they rest assured that the Spaniard and the Frenchman talk much faster than an American, and that they shall *never* talk French or Spanish at all. At the same time, they are determined, that when they can speak *tolerably well*, they will *begin*; like Paddy who had made up his mind not to bathe, 'till he knew how to swim They bar themselves from the only efficient mode of improvement, the habitual practice of speech right or wrong. Your first effort will no doubt extract an *occasional* smile; but foreigners, I must say, are far less inclined to ridicule, and far more ready to help out a tottering misconstructed sentence, than we are; and are well pleased to assist the beginner, by politely giving him any assistance required. By availing yourselves of opportunities and means, trifling in themselves, you may acquire a thorough knowledge of a language, without any expense, with scarcely any loss of time; at the same time forming useful and agreeable connections which you may find at all times ready and willing to serve you, merely because you can speak their language. I could give proofs numerous of this, but it would cost too much to print them. You will find more real friendship, and derive more advantage from a foreigner whose language you speak, than you can fairly expect from any other acquaintance.

Never be afraid to speak, because you fear to express your ideas rather awkwardly. Every time you give utterance to strange sounds, adds to your knowledge of pronunciation, and lessens your bashfulness, by giving you increased confidence in yourself. Always keep some study book in your pocket; you will find abundant opportunities for a few minutes study which (without any sacrifice of time) will not fail to amuse and instruct you.

Decide firmly on devoting so many minutes per day to study, be they ever so few; always pronounce what you read; thus, by accustoming yourself to the sounds, you will be better enabled to understand others.

Read every sentence over and over, until you can pronounce as fast as the same amount of English.

The daily learning of a little is peculiarly important in the study of a foreign language.

A small fire needs constant feeding.

Ten minutes per day, is one hour a week, and ten minutes study will cause an hour's reflection. One hour's study per week, a little every day, for one year, is often more than equal to six months lessons from a master. We always act with more decision, when we depend on ourselves rather than on the assistance of others. I do not mean to recommend my readers to study *only* one hour a week. Let them try the ten minutes per day, they will generally extend it, especially as they become more interested in the study. Any person of common abilities by studying one hour a day, in three months may make himself perfectly well understood, and as soon as he speaks a little, he receives an important and gratuitous lesson from all with whom he converses.

This is no fable; try it, you will succeed. You will find friends enough to solve all your difficulties.

By attending to a few general rules and analyzing

a few phrases, you will soon be able to compose for yourself, by noticing the forms of construction with which you have made *yourself* acquainted.

Suppose six persons agree to study one hour a day, to converse together whenever an opportunity offers; to meet together once a week, (or at any other stated periods) for the purpose of mutual instruction; to read, translate, converse, and solve difficulties among themselves. They would reap great advantage from this; for although there might be no great difference in their individual progress; still, as every one is studying on his "*own hook,*" each would have something new to communicate. Every difficulty should be noted down, to be unravelled the first favorable opportunity, by any person better informed than themselves. Learn a little here, a little there, read a little, write a little study a little, compose a little, talk a little. Don't make a task of it.

Keep a journal in Spanish of your daily transactions, the weather, remarkable events, etc. You need not be shy about this, as you will be the sole inspector of it, and day after day as you improve, you will be each day convinced of your progress, and daily correct your past errors. Five minutes per diem will suffice, and sometimes less. It is now 18 years that I have kept my journal in Spanish. For ten years I did not speak a half an hour in that language, but my Spanish recollections had been so continually aroused by my daily compositions (short as they were), that nothing was lost, and by dint of a few extra twists of the tongue I almost immediately recovered myself, and felt, in renewing my Spanish conversation, as though I had never been out of practice at all.

Mark well the construction of the phrases you read, and attempt the composition of others, in the same form, but of other materials.

I deem it unnecessary to enlarge much in Notes on difficulties in the conversations, as the student, by an attentive perusal, may easily analyze the sentences himself, and compose accordingly.

As soon as you have pronounced all the phrases thoroughly, look through on the Spanish side and see how much you can understand, always pronouncing aloud; and then look through on the English, translating it into Spanish: thus repeating the dose leisurely and cooly till you get thoroughly well versed in the facility of pronunciation, and well armed with a variety of conversational knowledge; then pursue the study just how, when, and where you please. If you don't succeed, call on the author and inform him of the fact, that he may note it down in his journal.

PRONUNCIATION
OF THE
SPANISH ALPHABET.

A, *ah*, always pronounced as in the words "thank, tank, flank, crank, tank Ex. *Casa Cama.*"

B, *bay*, same sound as in English.

C, *thay*, before the vowels a o u, sounded like K in English; at the end of the word or before a consonant like K.

C before i and e, like *th* in the English words *thin thatch*. *ch*. the same sound as in English.

D, *day*, as in English, but it must be pronounced very distinctly in the words terminating in ado, ido, &c. Ex. *duda, verdad.*

E, *ai*, always pronounced as e in the words bed, fed

F, *effe*, the same sound as in English.

G, *hay*, pronounced the same as in English before the vowels a o u; before e and i like the English aspirated *h* pronounced from the *throat*. Ex. *gefe, gitano.*

H. *atchay*, is never aspirated as in English, and may be said to be almost, if not wholly, silent.

I, *e*. always sounded like i in the English words "fit,

sit, pit," but more resembling the sound between the *i* in the last three, and the *ea* in the following: feat, seat, peat, not as long as feat, nor as short as fit.

J, *hota*, always has the same sound before all the vowels, as g has before e and i. Ex. *jarro, jesus, jornal, jugar.* (See G.)

K. No **K** in Spanish except in the spelling of foreign names.

L, *ellay*, the same sound as in English.

LL, *ellie*. Two ll's together always pronounced as in English in the word William.

M, *emay*, as in English.

N, *enay*, as in English; but at the end of a word has about half of the ringing sound in the English ng.

Ñ, *en-ye*, always sounded like *nni* in bie*nni*al, trie*nni*al.

O, *o*, the same sound as the o in the words "stone, bone," in English, but of about half the length.

P, *pay*, as in English.

Q, *koo*, the same sound as K, always accompanied, or rather followed by *u*.

R, *airy*. Be cautious in pronouncing this letter, you must give the Irish roll with the tongue, though very lightly, when it is single; except when beginning a word, or after a consonant; then strongly.

RR, *airry*. The r's when double are sounded very strong and rolling, like the r when used by an Irishman, *Arrah Pat.* &c.

S, *es*, always as in English in the words sit, sell, snow.

T, *tay*, as in English.

U, *oo*, precisely as the u in the words, *full, pull.*

V, *vay*, as in English. Ex. *valor, veo.*

W is found in no Spanish word; in foreign names is pronounced as in English.

X, *a kiss*, seldom found, and pronounced like "j" in Spanish, sometimes like x in English. This letter is almost out of use; *cs* is substituted for it.

Y, *egreaga*, pronounced always like *y* in yeast.

Z, pronounced like th in thick.

The pronunciation of the Spanish language is as easy as it is simple; in learning the alphabet you have learned nearly all.

Pronounce the following combinations thoroughly, giving them the alphabetical sound; repeat them over and over till you find them easy.

Ab, ac, ad, af, ag, aj, al, am, an, añ, ap, ar, arr, as at, av, ax, ay, az.

Eb, ec, ed, ef, eg, aj, el, em, en, eñ, ep, er, err es, et, ev, ex, ey, ez.

Ib, ic, id, if, ig, ij, il, im, in, iñ, ip, ir, irr, is, it, iv, ix, iy, iz.

Ob, oc, od, of, og, oj, l, om, on, oñ, op, or, orr os, ot, ov, ox, oy, oz.

Ub, uc, ud, uf, ug, uj, ul, um, un, uñ, up, ur, urr, us, ut, uv, ux, uy, uz.

Ba, be, bi, bo, bu.	Ja, je, ji, jo, ju.
Ca, ce, ci, co, cu.	La, le, li, lo, lu.
Da, de, di, do, du.	Ma, me, mi, mo, mu.
Fa, fe, fi, fo, fu.	Na, ne, ni, no, nu.
Ga, ge, gi, go, gu.	Ña, ñe, ñi, ño, ñu.
Ha, he, hi, ho, hu.	Pa, pe, pi, po, pu.

RULE.

Words of two syllables ending in a vowel, the emphasis is on the first, but not as in English where the second syllable is often scarcely audible. Every sound must be pronounced fearlessly and audibly. All words ending in a consonant, have the emphasis on the second, except *es* added for the plural. Should a deviation from this rule occur, the accent will point it out to the pupil.

Pronounce the following words, recollecting that they are all simple alphabetical sounds :

Capa, casa, cojo, pozo, jarro, raton, poco, loco, rio, frio, monte, caja, jorge, pero, perro, buscar, cojer, pillo, silla, niño, señal, llano, llevar, llave, cuando, cuello, queja, quita, quebrar, casco, comer, beber.

RULE.

In words of three syllables lay the emphasis on the second, unless the accent should indicate an exception, *cachuca, comida, caballo, cajita, muchacho, sábado, ochenta, pájaro, pizarra, madera, perrito, cáscara, perilla, bigotes, hermana, bastante, puerta, castillo, número, olvidé.**

---

* The emphasis is always on the last sylable of the first person of the perfect and future tenses.

RULE.

Words of four syllables have the emphasis on the third. The exceptions will be accented as they occur.

Ex. *divertido, solamente, fatigado, prefiero, Acapulco, muchachita, campanilla, sympatia, majadero agradable, muchísimo, fortúito meteoro.*

RULE.

Words of five sylables have the emphasis on the fourth. The exceptions will be accented as they occur.

Inteligencia, inhospitable, intempestivo, jocoserio, mezcladamente. octavario, orfebreria equilátero inmitable, obediencia inordinado, inhabitable.

RULE.

Words of six sylables have the emphasis on the fifth. The exceptions will be accented as they occur

Discolladamente, descontentadizo, efectivamente, espilorcheria, hieroglífico.

In fine, the emphasis is generally found on the last sylable but one, except words ending in consonants, when it is on the last; except S. when added for the plural—which does not change the emphasis; all other exceptions will be accented.

REMARKS.

As I may have to make remarks on some of the parts of speech, I will endeavor to give you rules for recognizing to what part of speech a word may belong.

The articles are *the, a* and *an ; the* is expressed in four ways in Spanish and must invariably be of the same gender as the noun to which it relates, as also *a* and *an* expressed in Spanish by *un uno, una.*

The Noun is known by its representing either person, place or thing, virtue or vice, &c.: man, New York, inkstand, patience, sin, &c.

The Pronoun is the representative of the noun, and relates to it, therefore must agree with it.

The Verb expresses action, being or suffering.

Adverb qualifies the Verb, answering to how, when and where. Ex. here, yesterday, properly, &c.

The Adjective tells what the noun is, and must always be of the same gender and number as the noun to which it relates : *un muchacno, una mujer, buen hombre, buena mujer hombres feos las mujeres feas.* *

---

* Passive past Participles take the gender and number of the nouns to which they relate, according to the rule of adjectives. No other participle is changeable. Ex.—*La carne está cocida* : The meat is boiled.

Adjectives ending in *o* in the masculine singular change *o* into *a* for the feminine singular, *o* into *os* for the masculine plural, *o* into *as* for the feminine plural. Adjectives ending in *e* do not change for the feminine singular, but take an *s* for the plural of both genders. Adjectives ending in *l* change only for the plural, adding *es* for both genders.

ARTICLES.

un, uno, una	a
el, la, los, las	the
lo (neuter)	the
del (de el)	of the
al (á el)	to the

Nouns in common use to be committed to memory.*

The table	La mesa
The wine	El vino
The knife	El cuchillo
The fork	El tenedor
The glass	El vaso
The spoon	La cuchara
The vinegar	El vinagre
The pepper	La pimienta
The brandy	El aguardiente
The water	El agua
The beer	La cerveza
The cider	La cidra

* I have introduced a general assortment of the leading words, that the pupil may at once compose for *himself* and practice therewith.

The meat	La carne
The soup	La sopa
The vegetables	Las legumbres
The potatoes	Las papas
The cabbage	Las verzas
The salt	La sal
The pitcher	El jarro
The chair	La silla
The fire	El fuego
The man-servant	El criado
The maid-servant	La criada
The plate	El plato
The sauce	La salsa
The butter	La mantequilla
The cheese	El queso
A piece	Un pedazo
A small piece	Un pedacito
The breakfast	El almuerzo
The dinner	La comida
The tea	El té
The supper	La cena
The salad	La ensalada
The cup	La taza
The bottle	La botella
The milk	La leche
The chocolate	El chocolate
The coffee	El café
The chicken	El pollo
The turkey	El pavo
The fish	El pescado
Hunger	El hambre
Thirst	La sed
Appetite	El apetito

The woman	La mujer
The man	El hombre
The boy	El muchacho
The girl	La muchacha
The American	El Americano
The Englishman	El Yngles
The Mexican	El Mejicano
The Frenchman	El Frances
The German	El Aleman
The house	La casa
The road	El camino
The pavement	El piso
The store	La tienda
The corner	La esquina
The Square or market	La plaza
The horse	El caballo
The cart	El carro
The carman	El carretero
The wheel	La rueda
The store-keeper	El tendero
The church	La yglesia
The boat	El bote
The ship	El buque
The steam-boat	El vapor
The butcher	El carnicero
The baker	El panadero
The shoe-maker	El zapatero
The tailor	El sastre
The watch-maker	El relojero
The jeweller	El joyero
The sailor	El marinero
The miner	El minero
The school-master	El maestro de escuela
The barber	El barbero

The money	El dinero
The gold	El oro
The silver	La plata
The iron	El hierro
The copper	El cobre
The steel	El acero
The segar	El tabaco
The river	El rio
The sea	La mar—el mar
The box	La caja
The basket	La canasta
The book	El libro
The paper	El papel
The pen	La pluma
The ink	La tinta
The cow	La vaca
The calf	El ternero
The sheep	El carnero
The bull	El toro
The field	El campo
The country	El campo
The wood	El bosque
The wheat	El trigo
The oats	La avena
The barley	La cebada
The Indian corn	El maiz
The pear	La pera
The apple	La manzana
The orange	La naranja
The plum	La ciruela
The cotton	El algodon
The wool	La lana
The coat	El vestido
The vest	El chaleco

The pantaloons	Los pantalones
The shirt	La camisa

VERBS.

Useful verbs arranged alphabetically, to be committed to memory—10 every day if you please.

To ache	Doler
To answer	Contestar
To ask	Preguntar
To bake	*Cocer en horno*
To beat	Pegar
To blow	Soplar
To bleed	Sangrar
To boil	*Hervir*
To borrow	*Pedir* prestado de
To blow one's nose	Sonarse
To break	Romper
To bring	*Traer*
To build	Batir
To buy	Comprar
To call	Llamar
To change	Cambiar
To come	*Venir*
To come down	Bajar
To consent	*Consentir*
To consult	Consultar
To cost	*Costar*
To cough	Toser
To count	Contar
To cry	Llorar
To cure	Sanar
To cut	Cortar
To dance	Baylar
To deny	Negar

To desire	Desear
To die	Morir
To dream	Soñar
To dress	Vestir
To drink	Beber
To eat	Comer
To enter	Entrar
To fall	Caer
To feed	Dar de comer
To feel	Sentir
To find	Hallar
To find out	Descubrir
To fish	Pescar
To follow	Seguir
To fry	Freir
To go	Ir
To go up	Subir
To go out	Salir
To go in	Entrar
To go off	Marcharse
To get money	Ganar dinero
To guard	Guardar
To guess	Creer
To heal	Sanar
To heat	Calentar
To hide	Esconder
To hush	Callar
To imitate	Imitar
To invent	Inventar
To joke	Chancear
To kill	Matar
To keep	Guardar
To know	Saber, conocer,

To last	Durar
To learn	Aprender
To lend	Prestar
To let	Alquilar
To light	*Encender*
To live	Vivir
To look	Mirar
To loosen	*Soltar*
To love	Amar, *querer*
To lose	*Perder*
To make	*Hacer*
To marry	Casarse
To melt	Fundir
To meet	*Encontrar*
To mend	*Enmendar*
To open	*Abrir*
To order	Mandar
To pass	Pasar
To pick up	Cojer
To play	*Jugar*
To pull	Tirar
To push	Empujar
To put	*Poner*
To read	*Leer*
To ride on horseback	Montar á caballo
To roast	Asar
To respect	Respetar
To sail	Poner á la vela
To save	Salvar
To saw	*Serrar*
To seduce	Seducir

* For the conjugation of verbs regular and irregular, see Verbs at the end of the dialogues.

To sell	Vender
To serve	Servir
To sew	Coser
To shave	Afeitar
To sign	Firmar
To sing	Cantar
To sleep	Dormir
To smoke	Fumar
To sow	Sembrar
To snow	Nevar
To stop	Parar
To suppose	Suponer
To sup	Cenar
To surprise	Sorprender
To swear	Jurar
To sweat	Sudar
To swim	Nadar
To wait	Esperar
To wake	Despertar
To walk	Andar
To wash	Lavar
To wish	Desear
To write	Escribir
To whistle	Silbar
To take	Tomar
To take away	Llevar
To talk	Hablar
To teach	Enseñar
To tear	Destruir
To teaze	Importunar
To tell	Decir
To tie	Amarrar
To think	Pensar

To throw	Echar
To translate	*Traducir*
To travel	Viajar
To treat	Tratar
To trust	Fiar
To use	Servirse de
To visit	Visitar

ADJECTIVES IN COMMON USE

Angry	Enfadado
Bad	Malo
Bitter	Amargo
Blind	Ciego
Blue	Azul
Brave	Valiente
Brown	Moreno
Cheap	Barato
Clean	Límpio
Cold	Frio
Cowardly	Cobarde
Damp	Húmedo
Dark	Oscuro
Dear	Caro
Dirty	Sucio
Dishonest	Pillo
Dry	Seco
Dumb	Mudo
Easy	Fácil
Empty	Vacio
Fat	Gordo
Fierce	Feroz
Fond	Aficionado
Generous	Generoso
Glad	Contento

USEFUL ADJECTIVES.

Good	Bueno
Great	Grande
Green	Verde
Guilty	Culpable
Hard	Duro
Hasty	Arrojado
High	Alto
Honest	Honrado
Innocent	Inocente
Jealous	Zeloso
Large	Grande
Lean	Flaco
Light	Claro
Little	Chico, pequeño
Long	Largo
Lovely	Amable
Low	Bajo
Mad	Loco, rabioso
Narrow	Estrecho
Naughty	Malo
Neat	Aseado
New	Nuevo
Nice	Bueno
Noisy	Ruidoso
Old	Viejo
Open	Abierto
Pleased	Contento
Polite	Politico
Poor	Pobre
Punctual	Exacto
Queer	Estraño
Quiet	Quieto
Raw	Crudo

USEFUL ADJECTIVES.

Red	Encarnado
Rich	Rico
Rough	Áspero
Round	Redondo
Saleable	Vendible
Sick	Malo
Sickly	Enfermizo
Short	Corto
Small	Chico
Soft	Suave
Sorry	Pesaroso
Sound	Sano, sólido
Strong	Fuerte
Sweet	Dulce
Tall	Grande, alto
Tender	Tierno
Thick	Espeso
Thin	Delgado
Tough	Duro
Ugly	Feo
Useful	Útil
Useless	Inútil
Variable	Variable
Weak	Débil
Well	Bueno
White	Blanco
Wide	Ancho
Wasteful	Pródigo
Young	Jóven.

PERSONAL PRONOUNS.

I	Yo
Me, to me	Me, á mí
Thou	Tú
Thee, to thee	Te, á tí

PERSONAL PRONOUNS.

He	Él
She	Ella
We	Nos, nosotros—as
You	Vos, vosotros—as
They	Ellos, ellas
Himself, herself,	
Themselves, itself,	Se
One's self,	
To himself, &c.	
They say, &c.	Se (dice)
Him to him	
To her, to it	Le
Her, *it*,	La (fem)
The one,	Él, la
The ones,	Los, las
With me	Conmigo
With thee	Contigo
One's self	Consigo
It	Lo

POSSESSIVE PRONOUNS.

	Singular	Plural.
My	Mi	Mis
Thy	Tu	Tus
His	Su	Sus
Our	Nuestro—a	Os—as
Your	*Vuestro—a	Os—as
Their	Su	Sus
Her	Su	Sus
Its	Su	Sus
Mine	S. El mio, la mia	
	P. *Los mios, la mias*	
Thine	S. El tuyo, la tuya	
	P. *Los tuyos, las tuyas*	

* Only used in the plural, and in speaking to Kings, etc.

His	S. El suyo, la suya
	P. *Los suyos, las suyas,*
Ours	S. El nuestro, la nuestra
	P. *Los nuestros, las nuestras*
Yours	S. El vuestro, la vuestra
	P. *Los vuestros, las vuestras*
Theirs	S. El suyo, la suya
	P. *Los suyos, las suyas*
Hers	S. El suyo, la suya
	P. *Los suyos, las suyas*
Your	S. El suyo, la suya
	P. *Los suyos, las suyas*

ADVERBS, &c.
Words used Adverbially.

Here	Aquí, acá
There	Allí, allá
However	
Nevertheless	Sinembargo
Somewhere	Alguna parte
Nowhere	Ninguna parte
Yonder	Allí
Any how	De cualquier modo
A long way off	Muy léjos
Under	Debajo
Over	Encima
Inside	Á dentro
Outside	Á fuera
Before	Ántes
Behind	Detras
Near	Cerca
Far	Léjos
Aside	De un lado

ADVERBS, ETC.

To the right	A la derecha
To the left	Á la izquierda
To-day	Hoy
Yesterday	Ayer
Pretty well	Así
To-morrow	Mañana
The day before yesterday	Ante ayer
The day after to-morrow	Pasado mañana
Next week	La semana que viene
Early	Temprano
Late	Tarde
This morning	Esta mañana
This afternoon	Esta tarde
This evening	Esta noche
To-night	Á noche
Next year	El año que viene
Always	Siempre
Immediately	Al instante
As soon as possible	Lo mas pronto posible
An hour ago	Hace una hora
In an hour	Dentro de una hora
Seldom	Rara vez
Often	Amenudo
Every day	Todos los dias
Lately	Hace poco
Now	Ahora
Then	Entónces
After	Despues
Before	Ántes
Soon	Pronto
By degrees	Poco á poco
Willingly	Con gusto
Nothing	Nada
On horseback	A caballo

ADVERBS, ETC.

On foot	Á pié
Well	Bien
Badly	Mal
Worse	Peor
Better	Mejor
On purpose	Á propósito
Much	Mucho
Little	Poco
At least	Á lo ménos
Enough	Bastante
Too much	Demasiado
More	Mas
Less	Ménos
Thus	Así
Scarcely	Á pénas
Besides	Ademas
Up side down	Al reves
Together	Juntos–as
Gently	Despácio
Right	Bien
Wrong	Mal
How	Como
When	Cuando
Where	Endonde, adonde
Why	Porqué
How long ago	Cuanto hace
Yes	Sí
No	No
Not yet	Todavia no
Perhaps	Puedeser
Certainly	Por supuesto
No doubt	Sin duda
To be sure	Ya se ve
Never	Nunca, jamas

And	Y
That	Que
Neither, nor	Ni, ni
Nor I either	Ni yo tampoco
Either	Ó
Or	Ó
Except	Sino que, á no ser que
But	Pero, mas
Because	Porque
Since	Pues, pues que
If	Si

Conjunctions, governing the Subjunctive

In order that	Para que, á fin que
Unless	A ménos que, á no ser que
Before	Antes que
In case	En caso que
Even	Aun cuando
Although	Aunque
Supposing that	Dado que
Providing that	Con tal que
Until	Hasta que
However	Por mas que

PREPOSITIONS.

To	Á
Before	Ante
With	Con
Against	Contra
Of	De
Since	Desde
In	En
Between	Entre
Towards	Hácia
As far as	Hasta
For, in order to	Para

PREPOSITIONS

By	Por
According	Segun
Without	Sin
On	Sobre
Behind	Detras

INTERJECTIONS,

Ah ! ay ! eh ! oh ! ola ! to ! chito ! ea ! sus ! tate !

The days of the week.   * Los dias de la Semana.

* Pronounce every sentence until it becomes easy ; if you pronounce with difficulty, it will be difficult to make you speak at all.

Sunday	Domingo
Monday	Lúnes
Tuesday	Mártes
Wednesday.	Miércoles
Thursday	Juéves
Friday	Viérnes
Saturday	Sábado

The Months — Los Meses

January	Enero
February	Febrero
March	Marzo
April	Avril
May	Mayo
June	Junio
July	Julio
August	Agosto
September	Setiembre
October	Octubre
November	Noviembre
December	Diciembre

The Numbers — Los Números

One	Uno
Two	Dos
Three	Tres
Four	Cuatro
Five	Cinco
Six	Seis
Seven	Siete
Eight	Ocho
Nine	Nueve
Ten	Diez

Eleven	Once
Twelve	Doce
Thirteen	Trece
Fourteen	Catorce
Fifteen	Quince
Sixteen	Diez y seis
Seventeen	Diez y siete
Eighteen	Diez y ocho
Nineteen	Diez y nueve
Twenty	Veinte
Twenty-one	Veinte y uno
Twenty-two, &c	Veinte y dos, &c
Thirty	Treinta
Thirty-one	Treinta y uno
Thirty-two, &c.	Treinta y dos, &c.
Forty	Cuarenta
Forty-one	Cuarenta y uno
Forty-two, &c.	Cuarenta y dos, &c.
Fifty	Cincuenta
Fifty-one	Cincuenta y uno
Fifty-two, &c	Cincuenta y dos, &c
Sixty	Sesenta
Sixty-one	Sesenta y uno
Sixty-two	Sesenta y dos
Seventy	Setenta
Seventy-one	Setenta y uno
Seventy-two, &c.	Setenta y dos, &c.
Eighty	Ochenta
Eighty-one	Ochenta y uno
Eighty-two	Ochenta y dos
Eighty-three, &c	Ochenta y tres, &c.
Ninety	Noventa
Ninety-one	Noventa y uno
Ninety-two, &c.	Noventa y dos, &c

A hundred	Ciento
A hundred and one	Ciento y uno
A hundred and two, &c.	Ciento y dos, &c
A thousand	Mil
Ten thousand	Diez mil
A million	Un millon
Ten millions	Diez millones
Eighteen hundred and forty seven	Mil ocho cientos Cuarenta y siete
New York, October 28th, 1847.	Nueva York, 28 de Octubre, de mil ocho cientos cuarenta y siete 1847.
First	Primero o primera
Second	Segundo a
Third	Tercero a
Fourth	Cuarto a
Fifth	Quinto a
Sixth	Sesto a
Seventh	Séptimo a
Eighth	Octavo, octava
Ninth	Noveno
Tenth	Décimo a
Eleventh	Undécimo a
Twelfth	Duodécimo a
Thirteenth	Décimotercio a
Fourteenth	Décimoquarto a
Fifteenth	Décimoquinto a
Sixteenth	Décimosesto a
Seventeenth	Décimoseptimo
Eighteenth	Décimooctavo
Nineteenth	Décimonono
Twentieth	Vigésimo a

NUMBERS

Twenty-first	Vigésimo-primero
Twenty-second	" segundo
Twenty-third	" tercero
Twenty-fourth	" quarto a
Twenty-fifth	" quinto a
Twenty-sixth	" Sesto a
Twenty-seventh	" Séptimo a
Twenty-eighth	" Octavo a
Twenty-ninth	" Nono a
Thirtieth	Trigésimo a
Thirty-first, &c.,	Trigésimo primero e
Fortieth	Cuadragésimo a
Forty-first &c.	Cuadragésimo primero etc
Fiftieth	Quincuagésimo a
Fifty-first, etc.	" Primero a
Sixtieth	Sesagésimo a
Sixty-first, etc.	" Primero a
Seventieth	Septuagésimo a
Eightieth	Octogésimo a
Eighty-first, etc.	" Primero a
Ninetieth	Nonagésimo a
Ninety-first, etc.	" Primero a
Hundredth	Centésimo
Hundred and first, etc	" Primero a
Thousandth	Milésimo a
Two thousandth	Dosmilésimos
Millionth	Millonésimo
Two millionths, etc.	Dos millonésimo
A couple	Un par
Half a dozen	Media docena
Two half dozens	Dos medias docenas
Three half dozens, etc.	Tres medias docenas etc
Eight days, or a week,	Una octava
Nine days of prayer	Una novena

4

Half a score	Una decena
A dozen	Una docena
Two dozen	Dos docenas
Three dozen, etc.	Tres docenas
A fortnight	Quince dias
A dozen and a half	Una docena y média
Two dozen and a half	Dos docenas y média
A score	Una veintena
A score and a half	Treinta, trentena
Two score	Cuarenta cuarentena
Two score and a half	Cincuenta
Three score	Sesenta
One thousand	Mil
Two thousand	Dos mil
Three thousand, etc.	Tres mil, etc.
The half	La mitad
The third	La tercera
One third	Una tercera
Two thirds, etc.	Dos terceras, etc.
The quarter, or the fourth	El cuarto, ó la cuarta parte
One quarter, or one fourth	Un cuarto, ó una cuarta parte
Two quarters, or two fourths, etc.	Dos cuartos ó dos cuartas partes
The fifth	El quinto ó la quinta
One fifth	Una quinta parte
Two fifths, etc.	Dos quintas, etc.
One sixth	Un sesto, ó sesta
Two sixths, etc.	Dos sestos
One seventh	Un séptimo
Two sevenths, etc.	Dos séptimos
One eighth	Un octavo
Two eighths, etc.	Dos octavos

Double	Doble
Triple	Triple
Four fold	Cuadruplo
Five fold	Quintuplo
Six fold, &c	Sestuplo
Hundred fold, &c	Centuplo

To have, affirmatively followed by an object	Tener, afirmativamente seguido de un objeto

I have a father	Yo tengo padre
Thou hast a mother	Tu tienes madre
He has a father-in-law	El tiene suegro
He has a mother-in-law	El tiene suegra
We have an uncle	Tenemos un tio
You have an aunt	Teneis una tia
They have a grandfather	Tienen abuelo
They have a grandmother	Tienen abuela
I have had a cousin	Yo he tenido un primo
Thou hast had a cousin	Has tenido un primo
He has had a brother	Ha tenido un hermano
She has had a sister	Ella ha tenido una hermana
We have had a son-in-law	Hémos tenido un yerno
You have had a daughter-in-law	V ha tenido nuera
They have had a grandson	Han tenido un nieto
They have had a granddaughter	Han tenido una nieta
I had a son	Yo tenia un hijo
Thou hadst a daughter	Tenias una hija
He had a nephew	Tenia un sobrino
She had a niece	Tenia una sobrina
We had a brother-in-law	Teníamos un cuñado

AFFIRMATIVELY.

You had a sister-in-law	Tenia V una cuñada
They had a companion	Tenian un compañero
They had a companion	Ellas tenian compañero
I had had ink	Habia tenido tinta
Thou hadst had bread	Habias tenido pan
He had had meat	Habia tenido carne
She had had books	Habia tenido libros
We had had feathers	Habiamos tenido plumas
You had had quills	V habia tenido plumas
They had had pens	Habian tenido plumas
They had had apples	Habian tenido manzanas
I had a slate	Tenia una pizarra
Thou hadst paper	Tu tenias papel
He had a knife	El tenia cuchillo
She had a pen-knife	Ella tenia cortaplumas
We had a fork	Nosotros teniamos tenedor
You had a spoon	Vosotros teniais cuchara
They had salt	Ellas tenian sal
They had pepper	Ellas tenian pimienta
I shall have an egg	Tendré un huevo
Thou wilt have eggs	Tendras huevos
He will have a wife	Tendrá muger
He will have a spouse	Tendrá esposa
She will have a husband	Tendrá marido
She will have a spouse	Tendrá esposo
We shall have butter	Tendrémos mantequilla
You will have cheese	Tendréis queso
They will have milk	Tendran leche
They will have cream	Ellas tendran nata
Let us have an ox	Tengamos un buey
Have some oxen	Tenga bueyes

To have, negatively followed by an object

Tener, negativamente seguido de objeto

NEGATIVELY.

I have no peaches	No tengo melocotones
Thou hast no strawberries	No tienes fresas
He has no sugar	No tiene azúcar
She has no beer	No tiene cerveza
We have no cider	No tenemos cidra
You have no coffee	V no tiene café
They have no tea	No tienen té
They have no water	No tienen agua
I have had no wine	No he tenido vino
Thou hast had no China	No has tenido loza
He has had no glasses	No ha tenido vasos
She has had no hat	No ha tenido sombrero
We have had no plates	No hemos tenido platos
You have had no soup	No habeis tenido sopa
They have had no cups	No han tenido tazas
They have had no dishes	No han tenido fuentes
I had no razors	Yo no tenia navajas
Thou hadst no children	Tú no tenías niños
He had no napkin	El no tenía servilleta
She had no shoes	Ella no tenia zapatos
We had no gloves	Nosotros no teníamos guantes
You had no gaiters	V no tenia botines
They had no boots	No tenian botas
They had no cloak	No tenian capa
I shall have no clothes	No tendré vestidos
Thou wilt have no hat	No tendras sombrero
He will have no handkerchief	No tendrá pañuelo
She will have no pencil	No tendrá lápiz
We shall have no boy	No tendrémos muchacho
You will have no spectacles	V no tendrá anteojos
They will have no swords	No tendran espadas

They will have no umbrellas	No tendran paraguas
I should have no waistcoat	No tendria chaleco
Thou wouldst have no watch	No tendrías reló
He would have no cravat	No tendria corbata
She would have no purse	No tendria bolsa
We should have no tobacco	No tendríamos tabaco
You would have no wig	No tendríais peluca
They would have no scissors	No tendrían tijeras
They would have no fans	Ellas no tendrian abanicos

To have, interrogatively followed by an object
Tener interrogativamente seguido de objeto

Have I a comb?	Tengo peine?
Hast thou a necklace?	Tiénes tú collar?
Has he a pin?	Tiene él alfiler?
Has she a parasol?	Tiene ella parasol?
Have we any ribands?	Tenémos nosotros cintas?
Have you a ring?	Tiene V sortija?
Have they any cloth?	Tiénen ellos paño?
Have they any veils?	Tiénen ellas velas?
Have I had muslin?	He tenido yo muselina?
Hast thou had a garden?	Has tenido tú jardin?
Has he had a chamber?	Ha tenido él cuarto?
Has she had a cat?	Ha tenido ella gato?
Have we had a carpet?	Hémos tenido alfombra?
Have you had a shop?	Habéis tenido tienda?
Have they had chairs?	Han tenido sillas?
Have they had pictures?	Han tenido pinturas?
Had I a drawing room?	Tenia salon?
Hadst thou a house?	Tenías casa?

INTERROGATIVELY. 43

Had he a key ?	Tenia llave ?
Had she a parlor ?	Tenia sala ?
Had we any shutters ?	Teníamos postigos ?
Had you any windows ?	Tenian ustedes ventanas ?
Had they any doors ?	Tenian puertas ?
Had they any stairs ?	Tenian escalera ?
Shall I have a bed ?	Tendré cama ?
Wilt thou have a broom ?	Tendras escoba ?
Will he have any candles ?	Tendrá velas ?
Will she have any boxes ?	Tendrá cajas ?
Shall we have a cloak ?	Tendrémos capa ?
Will you have curtains ?	Tendrás cortinas ?
Will they have a feather bed ?	Tendran cama de plumas ?
Will they have a looking-glass ?	Tendran espejo ?

To have, negatively and interrogatively followed by an object	Tener, negativa é interrogativamente seguido de objeto
Have I not a lamp ?	No tengo lámpara ?
Hast thou no library ?	No tiénes librería ?
Has it no lid ?	No tiene cubierta ?
Has she no screen ?	No tiene biombo ?
Have we no cook ?	No tenemos cocinero ?
Have you no cook-maid ?	No tiene V cocinera ?
Have they no fruit ?	No tienen fruta ?
Have they no servants ?	No tienen criados ?
Had I not an academy ?	No tenia academia ?
Hadst thou not a bank ?	No tenias banco ?
Had he no money ?	No tenia dinero ?
Had she no tickets ?	No tenia boletines ?
Had we no guineas ?	No teníamos guineas ?

Had you no music ?	No tenia vmd música ?
Had they no letters ?	No tenian cartas ?
Had they no scholars ?	No tenian discípulos ?
Shall I have no dogs ?	No tendré perros ?
Wilt thou have no horses?	No tendras caballos ?
Will he have no cows ?	No tendrá vacas ?
Will she have no hens ?	No tendrá gallinas ?
Shall we have no cats ?	No tendrémos gatos ?
Will you have no rabbits?	No tendrá vmd conejos ?
Will they have no turtles?	No tendran tortugas ?
Will they have no segars?	No tendran tabacos

To be, affirmatively — Ser, Estar, afirmativamente

I am accessible	Yo soy accesible -
Thou art active	Tú eres activo
You are powerful	V es poderoso
He is admirable	El es admirable
She is active	Ella es activa
We are alone	Estamos solos
You are agile	Sois ágiles
They are amusing	Son divertidos
I have been arrogant	Yo he sido arrogante
Thou hast been assiduous	Tú has sido asiduo
You have been thoughtful	V ha estado pensativo
He has been attentive	El ha estado atento
She has been attentive	Ella ha estado atenta
We have been austere	Nosotros hemos sido áusteros
You have been blunt	Vosotros habeis sido impolíticos
They have been careful	Ellos han sido cuidadosos
I was bald	Yo era calvo

AFFIRMATIVELY.

Thou wast busy	Tu estabas ocupado
You were peaceful	V era pacífico
He was certain	El estaba seguro
She was certain	Ella estaba segura
We were cheerful	Estábamos alegre
You were chilly	Estábais temblando de frio
They were christians	Ellos eran cristianos
They were christians	Ellas eran cristianas
I had been constant	Yo habia sido constante
Thou hadst been faithful	Habias sido fiel
You had been obstinate	V habia sido obstinado
He had been courageous	Habia sido valiente
She had been pretty	Habia sido linda
We had been credulous	Habíamos sido crédulos
You had been curious	Habíais sido curiosos
They had been detained	Habian sido detenidos
They had been exact	Habian sido ecsactos
I was diligent	Yo era diligente
Thou wast eager	Estábas deseoso
You were morose	V era moroso
He was dumb	Era mudo
She was dumb	Era muda
We were dissatisfied	Estábamos malcontentas
You were expeditious	Estábais corrientes
They were envious	Éran envidiosos
They were envious	Éran envidiosas
I had been extravagant	Habia sido estravagante
Thou hadst been honest	Habías sido honrado
You had been positive	V habia sido positivo
He had been false	Habia sido falso
She had been false	Habia sido falsa
We had been angry	Habíamos estado enfadados

AFFIRMATIVELY.

You had been fearful	Vosotros habíais estado llenos de miedo
They had been feverish	Habian estado acalenturados
They had been grave	Habian estado graves
I shall be good	Seré bueno
Thou wilt be good	Tú seras búeno
He will be firm	Será firme
We shall be graceful	Serémos graciosos
You will be ready	Estaréis listos
They will be ignorant	Seran ignorantes
I shall have been humane	Habré sido humano
Thou wilt have been just	Habras sido justo
You will have been proud	V habrá sido orgulloso
He will have been hoarse	Habrá estado ronco
We shall have been hoarse	Habrémos estado roncos
You shall have been idle	Habréis sido perezosos
They will have been good	Habran sido buenos
They will have been good	Habran sido buenas
I should be inattentive	Seria desatento
Thou wouldst be lost	Tu estarias perdido
You would be inattentive	V estaria desatento
He would be incredulous	El seria incrédulo
She would be indulgent	Ella seria indulgente
We should be infirm	Nosotros estaríamos enfermos
You would be innocent	V seria inocente
They would be insolent	Ellos serian insolentes
They would be insolent	Ellas serian insoléntes
Be obliging	Sea V cortes
Be indulgent	Sea indulgente
Let him be humble	Que sea humilde
Let us be joyful	Seamos alegres
Be laborious	Sed laboriosos

Let them be learned	Que sean sabios
That I may be liberal	Que sea liberal
That thou mayst be small	Que seas pequeño
That you may be sick	Que V esté malo
That he may be light	Que sea lijero
That she may be light	Que sea lijera
That we may be merry	Que seamos risueños
That you may be minute	Que sea V minucioso
That they may be ugly	Que sean feos
That they may be modest	Que sean modestos
That I might be negligent	Que fuese negligente
That thou might'st be bad	Que fueses malo
That you might be tanned	Que V fuese moreno
That it might be new	Que fuese nuevo
That it might be new	Que fuese nueva
That we might be poor	Que fuésemos pobres
That you might be rich	Que fuéseis ricos
That they might be old	Que fuesen viejos
That they might be old.	Que fuesen viejas

To be, negatively. — Ser, Estar, negativamente

I am not prudent	Yo no soy prudente
Thou art not sick	Tu no estas malo
You are not prompt	V no está pronto
You are not prompt	V no está pronta
He is not happy	El no es feliz
She is not unhappy	Ella no es infeliz
We are not suspected	No somos sospechados
You are not uneasy	No estais inquietos
They are not unfortunate	No son desdichados
They are not turbulent	No son turbulentas
I have not been ungrateful	No he sido ingrato

NEGATIVELY.

Thou hast not been great	No has sido grande
You have not been fat	V no ha sido gordo
He has not been unjust	No ha sido injusto
It has not been useful	No ha sido útil
It has not been violent	No ha sido violento
She has not been wicked	No ha sido mala
We have not been wise	No hemos sido sabios
You have not been worthy	No habeis sido dignos
They have not been deaf	No han sido sordos
They have not been clean	No han sido limpias
I was not happy	No era feliz
Thou was't not intelligible	Tu no eras inteligente
You were not accustomed	No estaba V acostumbrado
It was not vast	No era vasto
It was not yellow	No era amarilla
He was not affected	No era afectado
She was not old	No era vieja
We were not alone	No estábamos solos
You were not angry	V no estaba enfadado
They were not apparent	No eran aparentes
They were not fine	No eran hermosos
I shall not be captive	No estaré cautivo
Thou wilt not be correct	No serás correcto
You will not be cruel	V no será cruel
It will not be broad	No será ancho
It will not be damp	No estará húmedo
He will not be dead	No morirá
She will not be deaf	No será sorda
We shall not be deceitful	No serémos engañosos
You will not be dextrous	No seréis diestros
They will not be difficult	No seran difíciles
They will not be fine	No seran hermosas
Be not dishonest	No seas pícaro

Be not disorderly	No seas desordenado
Let it not be excessive	Que no sea escesivo
Let it not be stiff	Que no sea tieso
Let it not be exempt	Que no sea ecsento
Let her not be admitted	Que no sea admitida
Let us not be liars	No seamos mentirosos
Be not insensible	No se dais insensibles
That they may not be fit	Que no sean aptos
That they may not be rich	Que no sean ricas
That they may not be wet	Que no esten mojados
That they may not be wet	Que no esten mojadas

To be Interrogatively	Ser y estar Interrogativamente.

Am I loyal?	Soy leal?
Art thou pensive?	Estas pensativo?
Art thou mortal?	Eres mortal?
Is he profound?	Es profundo?
Is she pompous?	Es pomposa?
Is it clean?	Está limpio?
Is it great?	Es grande?
Are we ridiculous?	Somos ridículos?
Are you respectful?	Sois respectuosas?
Are they revengeful?	Son vindicativos?
Are they hard?	Son duros?
Have I been romantic?	He sido romántico?
Hast thou been roguish?	Has sido pícaro?
Have you been patient?	Ha sido V paciente?
Has it been resolved?	Ha sido resuelto?
Has it been overturned?	Ha sido trastornado?
Has he been riotous?	Ha sido sedicioso?
Have we been furious?	Hemos estado furiosas?
Have we been sad?	Hemos estado tristes?

Have you been satirical?	Han sido Vs satíricos?
Have they been saving?	Han sido económicos?
Have they been senseless?	Han sido insensibles?
Shall I have been lost?	Habré estado perdido?
Wilt thou have been just?	Habras sido justo?
Will you have been serious?	V habrá sido serio?
Will he have been stiff?	Habrá sido tieso?
Shall we have been silly?	Habrémos estado locos?
Will you have been silly?	Habréis estado locas?
Will they have been full?	Habran sido llenos?
Will they have been full?	Habran sido llenas?
Should I be ridiculous?	Seria ridículo?
Wouldst thou be ashamed?	Tendrias vergüenza?
Would he be worthy?	Seria digno?
Should we be frank?	Seríamos francos?
Should you be blind?	Seria V ciego?
Should they be lame?	Serian cojos?

To be, Negatively and Interrogatively.
Ser y estar negativamente é interrogativamente.

Am I not tall?	No soy grande?
Art thou not pleased?	No estas contento?
Are you not covetous?	No es V avaro?
Is he not diffuse?	No es difuso?
Is she not detained?	No está detenida?
Is it not hard?	No es duro?
Is it not round?	No es redondo?
Are we not docile?	No somos dóciles?
Are you not humble?	No sois humildes?
Are they not hollow?	No estan huecos?
Have I not been furious?	No he estado furioso?
Hast thou not been glad?	No ha estado V contento?

NEGATIVELY.

Has she not been hoarse?	No ha estado ronca?
Have we not been hostile?	No hemos estado hostiles?
Have you not been sad?	No habeis estado tristes?
Have they not been heavy?	No han sido pesados?
Have they not been rivals?	No han sido rivales?
Was I not sincere?	No era sincero?
Wast thou not busy?	No estabas ocupado?
Were you not fearful?	No estábais medrosos?
Was he not curious?	No era curioso?
Was she not discreet?	No era discreta?
Were we not glad?	No estábamos alegres?
Were you not envious?	No estábais invidiosos?
Were they not expert?	No eran expertos?
Were they not skilful?	No eran diestros?
Was I not firm?	No estaba firme?
Wast thou not fantastical?	No eras fantástico?
Were you not just?	No era V justo?
Was he not ingenious?	No era ingenioso?
Was she not proud?	No estaba orgullosa?
Were we not slow?	No éramos tardios?
Were you not heavy?	No era V pesado?
Were they not frugal?	No eran frugales?
Were they not careful?	No eran cuidadosos?
Shall I not be despised?	No seré despreciado?
Wilt thou not be pleased?	No estaras contento?
Will you not be arrived?	No habrá V llegado?
Will he not be welcome?	No será bien venido?
Will she not be ready?	No estará lista?
Will it not be strong?	No será fuerte?
Will it not be long?	No será larga?
Shall we not be rich?	No serémos ricos?
Will you not be lame?	No estaréis cojos?
Will they not be punished?	No seran castigados?
Will they not be punished?	No seran castigadas?

Have you not been guilty?	No ha sido V culpable?
Has it not been tall?	No ha sido grande?

Titles. — Títulos.

Sir or gentleman	Señor, ó caballero
Sirs or gentlemen	Señores ó caballeros
A lady	Una Señora
Madam	Señora
Some ladies	Algunas* señoras
Ladies	Señoras
A young lady	Una señorita
Miss	Señorita
Some young ladies	Algunas señoritas
Misses or young ladies	Señoritas

To ask questions. — Para *hacer* preguntas

What is that?	Que es eso?
What is it?	Que es?
How do you call that?	Como se llama† eso?
What is the name of this?	Cual es el nombre de esto?
That is called . .	Eso se llama . .
What is the Spanish of . .	Como se dice . . en Español?
Tell me the Spanish of this word	Dígame como se dice esta palabra en Español
May I ask you if .	Me *hace* V el favor de decirme si . .

---

* Pronouns, articles and adjectives must be of the same gender and number as the nouns to which they relate.

† Reflected verb, always accompanied by the personal pronoun, either direct or indirect, as in English, "She poisoned herself. &c.

‡ The personal pronoun, the object of the verb, whether direct or indirect, is placed after the verb in the infinitive, and imperative affirmation· if otherwise before it

QUESTIONS.

May I take the liberty of asking you if . . .?	Permítame V§ preguntar le si. . . ?
May I trouble you to . . .?	Quiere V darse la pena de?
What do you wish to have?	Que desea V ?
What do you wish to have?	Que quiere V ?
What do you want ?	Que le‖ falta á V ?
Do you understand me ?	Me entiende V ?
Do you hear me ?	Entiende V ?
Do you not understand me?	No me entiende¶ ?
Yes, I do.	Sí le entiendo.
Yes, sir.	Sí Señor.
No, I do not.	No entiendo.
No, sir.	No Señor.
Do you understand what I say to your brother ?	Entiende V lo que le digo á su hermano ?
I understand very well what you say?	Entiendo bien lo que V le dice.
Will you be so good as to repeat what you said ?	Tenga V la bondad de* repetir lo que ha dicho ?
Will you be good enough to say it again ?	Me hace V el favor de decirlo otra vez ?
What do you say ?	Que *dice* V ?
Why do you not answer ?	Porqué no contesta V ?
Why do you not answer instantly ?	Porqué no contestas† al instante

§ V. abreviation of Vuestra Merced, (your grace) pronounced usted, and third person singular. In referring to V the him, or himself, her or herself must be expressed by le, to her him or to him, himself or to himself, la, her le, to her, se herself or to herself.

‖ Le and V are both used together in speaking respectfully. 'What to him lacketh, to your worship ?" Que le falta a V !

¶ V may be often omitted in familiar conversation.

* After any preposition, the verb must be in the infinitive.

† The second person tu, thou is used when very familiar with a person ; between school-boys and children, parents and children: as bespeaking affection ; also to express disdain, and in addressing animals. The nominative pronoun is seldom expressed in Spanish ex-

QUESTIONS.

Who told you that?	Quien le *dijo* eso?
Who told you so?	Quien se lo *dijo*?
What are you doing?	Que *hace* V?
What do you ask for?	Qué preguntas?
Whom do you ask for?	A quién solicita?
What is that good for?	Para qué es bueno eso?
What is the use of that?	Para qué sirve eso?
What do you want of me?	Para qué me quiere V?
What does that mean?	Que quiere decir eso?
What is the matter?	Que hay?
Are you sure of that?	Está V seguro de eso?
Inquire about that?	Infórmese V de eso.
Where are you going to?	A donde *va* V?
Whence do you come?	De donde *viene* V?
Where are they?	Endonde estan?
What ails that man?	Que padece ese hombre?
Whose stick is this?	De quien es este baston?
Whose books are these?	De quien son estos libros
Did you hear that?	Oyó V eso?
What do you want him for?	Para que le *quiere* V?
What do you want to say?	Que *quiere* V decir?
Do you know the news?	Sabe V las noticias?
What is the news?	Qu noticias hay?
Have you seen the newspapers?	Ha *visto* V los papeles?
Is there any news?	Hay algunas noticias?
What is the best news?	Que buenas noticias hay?
Will you come with me?	Quiere V *venir* con migo?
Where do you wish to go?	A donde *quiere* V ir?

cept when we lay an emphasis on it in English as, *I* would not go, *he* did.

‡ In a question, if the nominative be a Noun, it must follow the verb, and not be placed between the auxiliary and past participle

QUESTIONS.

Which way shall we go?	De que lado *irémos*?
What shall we do?	Que harémos?
What is to be done?	Que se ha de hacer?
What is to be done?	Que hay que hacer?
What course will you take in that affair?	De que médio se valdrá V en ese negócio
What have we to do?	Que tenemos que hacer?
I know not what to do.	No sé que hacer
What do you advise me to do?	Que me aconseja V que haga? §
What would you do in this case?	Que haria V en este caso?
Were I in your place ..	Si estubiera en su lugar..
What do you say to it?	Que le parece á V?
What do you think of it?	Que le parece á V de eso?
Is the master come?	Llegó el maestro?
Has he given it to him?	Se lo ha dado á él?
Does he understand?	Entiende?
Do you doubt it?	Lo duda V?
What are you thinking about?	En que esta V pensando? ‖
How far do you go?	Hasta donde va V?
Is he gone?	Se marchó? ¶
Are you going there? ·	Va V allá?
How many pupils are there?	Cuantos discípulos hay?

§ In doubt, supposition or when a future time is understood, the verb depending on another is generally in the subjunctive, preceded by *que*.

‖ The present participle, as in English, is used to denote the immediate presence of the act. Estoy comiendo, I am dining.

¶ The perfect tense is used to imply an act fully completed, at a fixed period

Is the door open?	Lapuerta está abierta?
Are the windows shut?	Están cerradas las ventanas?
How much do I owe you?	Cuanto le debo á V?
How much wine have you?	Tiene V mucho vino?
How many books have you?	Cuantos libros tiene V?
Whom is it for?	Para quién es?
What must I give?	Cuanto debo dar?
Did you speak to him?	Le habló V?
Are you going home?	Va V á casa?
When will you come?	Cuando vendrá V?
What do you wish me to do?	Que quiere V que haga?
When do you set out for Washington?	Cuando se marcha V para Washington?
Will you be home to-night?	Volverá V á la noche?
Do you wish to have it?	Lo quiere V?
Will you sell it me?	Me lo quiere V vender?
How much will you give me for it?	Cuanto me da V por esto?
How much do you want for it?	Cuanto pide V por esto?
Will you send it me?	Me lo quiere V enviar?

To salute and inquire after the health of some person.

Para saludar y preguntar por la salud de alguna persona

Good morning, sir	Buenos dias, señor
Good morning, gentlemen	Buenos dias, señores
Good morning, madam	Buenos dias, señora
Good morning, ladies	Buenos dias, señoras
Good morning, miss	Buenos dias, señorita

QUESTIONS AND ANSWERS.

Good morning young ladies	Buenos dias, señoritas, ú los pies de ustedes señoritas.
Good evening, sir, &c.	Buenas tardes, señor.
Good night, sir, &c.	Buenas noches, señor
I wish you good morning, sir, &c.	Buenos dias tenga V, señor, &c.
How do you do?	Como está V?
I am very well, thank you.	Bueno, muchas grácias.
I am very glad to see you in good health.	Me alegro mucho verle á V en buena salud.
I am very happy to see you.	Me alegro de verle.
How is your father?	Como está su padre?
He is very well, I thank you.	Muy bueno, gracias.
And, how are your sisters?	Y como estan sus hermanas de V?
They are tolerably well.	Bastante buenas.
How are they all at home?	Como estan todos en casa?
How does all the family do?	Como está toda la familia?
Every body is very well.	Todos estan buenos.
You do not look well.	V parece no estar buena.
Are you sick?	Está V malo?
I am not very well.	No me siento may bueno
I am not in very good health.	No tengo muy buena salud.
I feel indisposed.	Me siento indispuesto.
I do not feel comfortable.	No me siento bueno
I suffer a great deal.	Padezco mucho.
I have been obliged to keep my bed.	He tenido que guardar cama.
I have had a bad cold.	He estado muy constipado

I have had a little fever.	He tenido un poco* de fiebre.
I have had a shivering the whole night.	He estado temblando toda la noche.
I did not sleep a wink.	No he cerrado los ojos toda la noche.
I have had a cold for several days.	Hace dias que estoy constipado.
I have a very bad cough.	Tengo mucha tos.
I am a little better this morning.	Me siento un poco mejor, esta mañana.
I feel greatly relieved.	Me siento muy aliviado.
I have had the headache.	He tenido dolor de cabeza.
I have had a sore throat.	He tenido dolor de garganta.
I am hoarse.	Estoy ronco.
I have a cold in my head.	Tengo catarro.
I hope it will be nothing.	Espero que pronto se restablecerá.
I have the toothache.	Tengo dolor de muelas.
I hope you will soon get over it.	Espero que le pasará pronto
I am very sorry for your indisposition.	Siento mucho su indisposicion.
Your illness grieves me exceedingly.	Me aflige mucho su indisposicion.
We must hope it will have no bad consequence.	Debemos de esperar que no tendrá mala consecuencia.
Your brother seems very well	Su hermano parece bueno.

---

* Little, when meaning small, must be expressed by perqueño chi
the Poco adjective means few ; when an adverb, a little.

He possesses a very strong constitution.	Tiene una constitucion muy fuerte.
His son appears to have delicate health.	Su hijo parece tener mala salud.
I do not think he will live long.	No creo que viva mucho tiempo.
Advise him to go into the country.	Aconséjele que vaya al campo.
He will enjoy there better health than in the city.	Allí gozará de mejor salud que en la ciudad.
He might recover by dint of care.	A fuerza de cuidado puede restablecerse.

Getting up. — Al levantarse.

Up, Up!	Arriba ! arriba !
Rise, get up!	Levántese V.
How sleepy you are!	Que sueño tiene!
Let me sleep?	Déjeme dormir.
It is yet too early to get up.	Es demasiado temprano para levantarse.
Too early!	Demasiado temprano !
Yes, too early.	Sí demasiado temprano
Do you know what o'clock it is?	Sabe V que hora es?
It cannot be late.	No puede ser tarde.
It may be five o'clock.	Las cinco, acaso.
Five o'clock! it is after Eight.	Las cinco! pasa de las ocho.
I did not think it was so late	No creia que era tan tarde
Come down quickly.	Baje V pronto.
I am going to get up directly.	Me voy á levantar ahora mismo.
Make haste to dress yourself.	Vistase pronto

I shall not be long dressing myself.	No tardaré mucho en vestirme.
You should be at school by this time.	Ya debia estar en la escuela á esta hora.
Your companions are already in the yard.	Ya estan tus compañeros en el patio.
They are more diligent than you	Son mas diligentes que tú
It is not my fault.	No es culpa mia.
Nobody woke me.	Nadie me despertó.
You have been called twice.	Le han llamado á V. dos veces.
You go to bed too late.	V. se acuesta demasiado tarde.
I must rise to-morrow by day-break.	Mañana tengo que levantarme al amanecer.
At what o'clock do you rise?	A que hora se levanta usted?
I rise at six o'clock.	Me levanto á las seis.
It is too early.	Es demasiado temprano.
I like to rise early.	Me gusta levantarme temprano.
My health improves by it.	He mejorado mucho de salud.

To dress one's self.

Para vestirse.

John, make a fire in my room.	Juan enciende el fuego en mi cuarto.
Warm a little water.	Calienta un poco de agua
Give me my morning gown	Dame mi bata.

TO DRESS ONE'S SELF.

Give me a pair of white silk stockings.	Dame un par de medias de seda blancas*
Bring me my shoes.	Tráygame mis zapatos.
Are they properly cleaned?	Estan bien limpios?
They are badly blacked.	No tiénen lustre
Clean them better than that.	Límpielos mejor de lo que estan.
Pour some warm water into this basin.	Eche agua caliente en esa palangana.
I wish to wash my hands.	Quiero lavarme†las manos
Give me some cold water to wash my face.	Tráheme agua fria para lavarme la cara.
Where is the soap?	Endonde está el jabon?
Bring me my razors.	Tráygame mis navajas.
My scissors do not cut.	Mis tijeras no cortan
My linen is damp.	Mi ropa está húmeda.
Dry it a little,	Séquela un poco.
Has the washerwoman brought my linen?	La lavandera ha traido mi ropa?
Is nothing wanting?	No falta nada?
Where is her bill?	Endonde está su cuenta?
Pay her all I owe her since she washes for me.	Páguele todo lo que debo desde que lava mi ropa.
Give me a neckcloth.	Deme una corbata.
Have I got a white handkerchief?	No tengo pañuelo blanco?
Brush my hat.	Cepílleme el sombrero.
Where are my gloves?	Endonde estan mis guantes?

---

* El sombrero de Juan, John's hat. El camino de hierro, the railroad, una casa de madera, a wooden house, &c

† In speaking of any part of the person, the possessive pronoun is not used; but say Me lavé la cara. Lo corté el dedo. To myself I washed the face, to him I cut the finger.

I cannot find them.	No puedo encontrarlas.
Look for them.	Búsquelos
They cannot be lost.	No pueden estar perdidos.
I had them last evening when I came home.	Los tenia cuando volvi ayer noche.
Go and fetch me a towel.	Vaya á buscarme una toalla.
You have put on your stockings wrong side out.	V. ha puesto las medias al reves.
Take this coat to the tailor's.	Lleve esta levita al sastre.
Tell him to put a new lining to it.	Dígale que le ponga forro nuevo.
This waistcoat wants several buttons.	Faltan algunos botones á este chaleco.
These shoes have no strings.	Estos zapatos no tienen cordones.
Do you wish for a pin?	Quiere V un alfiler?
Give me a needle.	Deme una aguja.
Whose hat is this?	De quien es este sombrero?
It is not mine.	No es mio.
Here is yours.	Aquí está el suyo.*
Where was it?	Endonde estaba?
That hat fits you well.	Le está bien ese sombrero.
It is too narrow.	Es demasiado chico.
These boots are too large.	Estas botas son demasiado anchas.
These boots pinch me too much.	Estas botas me apriétan mucho, ó (lastiman).
The cloth of this coat is very fine.	El paño de esta levita es muy fino.

---

* V being the third person, the pronouns relating to it must be in the third person. su, suyo, suya, se lo. Su, may mean his, her, its, their, your. Suyo a, his, hers, its, theirs, yours. Se, himself, one's self, herself, itself, themselves. Le, him, you, to him, to you, to her

ASKING AND THANKING.

I want a coat	Quiero una levita.
Show me some cloth.	Déjeme ver paño.
This blue cloth pleases me pretty well.	Este paño azul* me gusta bastante
Take my measure.	Tomeme V. medida.
This coat fits you well.	Me está bien esta casaca.
It is very well made.	Está† muy bien hecha.
This coat is out of fashion.	Esta casaca ya no es de moda.
I like to be neatly and plainly dressed.	Me gusta vestir aseado y sencillo.
Her dress is very becoming to her.	Su túnico le va muy bien.
He dresses after the English fashion.	Se viste á la Ynglesa.
Make me a fashionable waistcoat.	Hágame un chaleco de moda.
In summer I like to wear gaiters.	En verano me gusta traer botines.
How much will you charge me for a coat?	Cuanto tendré que pagar por una casaca?
That is too dear for a summer coat.	Es demasiado caro para una casaca de Verano.
When will it be done?	Cuando se acabará.
You shall have it on next Saturday without fail.	La tendrá V. el Sábado sin falta.

Asking and Thanking.	Para preguntar y dar gracias.
With your leave.	Con el permiso de V.
Will you give me leave to * * * *?	Me permite V.

* The adjectives are generally placed after the noun
† Distinguished from the pronoun by the accent.

ASKING AND THANKING.

Do me the pleasure of * * * ?	Hágame* V. el favor de * * * ?
Will you have the goodness to * * * ?	Tenga V la bondad de * *;
Will you be so kind as to * * * ?	Me hace V el favor de * ?
I have a favor to ask of you.	Tengo que pedir le á V un favor ?
I should have a favor to ask you.	Tendria que pedirle á V un favor.
I have a favour to beg of you.	Tengo un favor que pedirle á V
May I beg a favor of you ?	Permítame V que le pida un favor.
Will you do me a favour ?	Me quiere V hacer un favor ?
Will you render me a service ?	Me hace V un servício ?
You can render me a great service.	V puede hacerme un servício ?
You could render me a great service.	V. podria hacerme un gran servício.
I shall do it if I can.	Lo haré con tal que pueda.
I would do it if I could.	Lo haría, si pudiera.
I shall be much obliged to you.	Le estaré muy obligado.
I am very much obliged to you.	Le† doy á V mil grácias.
I am greatly indebted to you	Le debo á V mucho.

---

* When the personal pronoun is after the verb it is joined to it.

† When a person is the object of a verb, either direct or indirect, á precedes the person or pronoun representing that person. Lo veo á V. I see you. Not so with regard to things

I am extremely indebted to you.	Le debo á V muchísimo.*
I thank you most kindly.	Le doy á V mil gracias
I thank you.	Gracias.
I thank you with all my heart.	Le agradezco á V muchísimo.
It is not worth mentioning, you jest.	No vale la pena; V se chancea.
I give you much trouble.	Molesto a V. mucho.
I give you too much trouble.	Le incomodo demasiado.
You take a great deal of trouble.	V. se molesta mucho.
I am sorry to trouble you so much.	Siento mucho molestar á V tanto.
I am ashamed of the trouble I give you.	Siento darle á V tanta molestia.
No trouble at all.	Nada de eso.
I beg you would not mention it.	Le suplico á V que no hable mas de eso.
Do not mention that, you are very kind.	No hable V de eso, V es muy atento.
You are very civil, sir.	Señor, es V. muy político.
I shall remember all my life the service you have just done me.	Me acordaré toda la vida del servicio que V me ha hecho.

To Consult.

Para Consultar.

What is to be done?	Que se ha de hacer?
What course shall we take?	Que medio tomarémos?

---

* Isimo is the superlative in Spanish, and may be added to almost any adjective to indicate a great quantity &c.

What course remains for us to take?	Que nos queda que hacer?
What shall we do?	Que harémos?
What have we to do?	Que tenémos que hacer?
What are we to do?	Que hay que hacer?
What remains for us to do now?	Que nos queda que hacer?
Let us see if you please.	Veamos si V gusta.
We must resolve upon something.	Es preciso decidir algo.
We must take some course	Es preciso tomar algun partido.
I am quite puzzled.	Estoy confundido.
I do not know what to do.	No sé* que hacer.
I am in a great embarrassment.	Estoy muy apurado.
We are in a great dilemnia.	Estamos entre la espada y la pared.
We are in a very perplexing case.	Nos hallamos en un caso muy estrecho.
Were I you.	Si fuera V.
Were I in your place.	Si estubiera en su lugar.
I advise you to....	Le aconsejo que
I am of opinion that you should go there.	Me parece que V debe ir allá.
If you will take my advice you will do it.	Si V quiere tomar mi consejo, lo hará.
An idea strikes me.	Me ocurre una idea.
I have been thinking of one thing.	He pensado en una cosa
A thought has struck me	Me vino una idea.
Let me alone.	Déjeme.
Let us do one thing.	Hagamos una cosa
I have altered my opinion	He mudado de parecer.

* Distinguished from the pronoun by the accent.

I have altered my mind.	He mudado de opinion
Let us do otherwise.	Hagamos otra cosa.
Let us go another way to work.	Tomemos otro camino.
What do you say about it?	Que dice V de eso?
What do you think of it?	Que le parece á V?
I think as you do.	Yo soy del mismo parecer
It is very well thought.	Está bien pensado.
It is very well imagined.	Está bien concebido.
This is a good thought.	Es buena idea.
This is a very good idea.	Es muy buena idea.
I am of your opinion.	Estoy de su parecer.
It is the best way.	Es el mejor modo.
Would it not be better?	No seria mejor?
It is the best we can do.	Es lo mejor que podemos hacer.
It is the best thing we can do	Es la mejor cosa que podemos hacer.
It is the only thing we have to do.	No hay otra cosa que hacer.
That is the only course we can take.	Es el solo camino que podemos tomar.

To affirm and deny. — Para afirmar y negar.

I am going to tell you that....	Voy á decirle á vmd que....
I assure you that...	Le aseguro que...
I warrant it.	Lo garantizo.
That I assure you.	Eso, lo aseguro.
That I can assure you.	Eso, lo puedo asegurar
I could not answer for it.	Yo no lo garantizo

Rely upon what I tell you.	Cuente V en lo que digo.
I maintain that it is so.	Sostengo que es así.
I say it is.	Yo digo que sí.
I say it is not.	Yo digo que no.
I lay it is.	Yo apuesto que sí.
I lay it is not.	Yo apuesto que no.
I suppose so.	Lo supongo.
You may well think that	Bien puede V creer que..
You may easily think that.	V puede facilmente concebir que.,.
Do you think so?	Lo cree vmd?
I think so.	Lo creo.
I think so too.	Yo lo creo tambien.
I do not think so.	Yo no lo creo.
You must know. .	Debe vmd saber....
I must tell you....	Debo decirle á vmd....
I have a notion that....	Tengo una idea de que...
I am inclined to think....	Me inclino á creer.
I dare say it is so.	Sin duda que es así.
What do you mean?	Que quiere vmd decir?
I do not know what you do mean.	No sé lo que vmd quiere decir.
Is it certain that...?	Es cierto que...?
Is it true that....?	Es verdad que...?
Yes, it is true.	Sí, es verdad
Yes, that is certain.	Sí, eso es cierto.
It is but too true.	Es demasiado cierto.
It is a fact.	Es un hecho.
It is an absolute fact.	Es hecho positivo.
Are you sure of what you say?	Está vmd seguro de lo que dice?
Would you believe that...	Creeria vmd que....

* When *what* means "that which," it must be expressed by *lo que*.

AFFIRM AND DENY

I could believe it	Podria creerlo.
Do you believe it?	Lo cree vmd?
I believe it truly.	En verdad que lo creo.
I believe so too.	Creo lo mismo.
That I believe.	Eso, lo creo.
I do not believe anything of it.	No creo nada de eso.
I do not believe a word of it.	No creo una palabra de eso.
I think so.	Lo creo.
I do not think so.	No lo creo.
I make no doubt of it.	No lo dudo.
Are you quite sure of it?	Está vmd seguro de eso?
Nothing is more certain.	Nada es mas cierto.
I answer for it.	Yo lo garantizo.
I do not believe it.	Yo no lo creo.
You may believe me.	Puede V creerme.
It cannot be true.	No puede ser verdad.
It is a story.	Es cuento.
It is an invention.	Es una invencion.
I protest that....	Protesto que.
Upon my honour	Palabra de honor.
Upon my word of honor.	Le doy á V mi palabra de honor.
It is really true?	Es verdad, (de veras).
I can hardly believe it.	Apénas puedo creerlo.
I heard it said by a credible person.	Lo he oido decir á una persona de confianza.
We must not always give credit to all we hear people say.	No hemos de creer siempre todo lo que se dice.*

---

* Se is used as an indefinite nominative. Se dice, it is said.

Going to School.

Going to School.	Para ir á la Escuela.
I must go to school.	Es menester que vaya á la Escuela.
I am afraid to be too late.	Temo que sea demasiado tarde.
Where are my books?	Endonde estan mis libros?
Where did you put them last night?	Endonde los pusiste ayer noche?
I do not know, mother.	No sé mamá.
Why do you not put them always together in the same place?	Porqué no los pones siempre juntos, en su lugar?
You would not have so much trouble to find them every morning.	Ne tendrias tanto trabajo en encontrarlos todas las mañanas.
You have no order.	No tienes órden.
I hope your master will punish you.	Espero que tu maestro te castigará.
I will not give you any excuse.	No te daré escusa ninguna.
I shall tell it your father when he comes in.	Lo diré á tu padre cuando venga.
He will punish you also.	Te castigará tambien.
You must absolutely have order.	Has de tener órden absolutamente.
If you are not forced to it now, you will never have any.	Si ahora por fuerza no te lo ponen, no lo tendrás nunca.
John, Mary, did you see my grammar?	Juan, María, habeis visto mi gramática.
It is in the dining-room, under the table.	Está en el salon bajo la mesa.

GOING TO SCHOOL.

Mary where is my copy-book?	María, endonde está mi borrador.*
I saw it on a chair.	Lo vi. en la silla.
I do not know where.	No sé endonde.
I think it was in your bed-room.	Me parece que estaba en tu cuarto.
John, Mary, Joseph, where is my hat?	Juan, María, José endonde está mi sombrero?
Here it is in the yard.	Aquí está en el patio.
Why do you come so late?	Porque viénes tan tarde?
I could not come sooner, sir.	Señor, no he podido venir mas temprano.
What detained you?	Que le retardó?
I could not have my breakfast sooner.	No pude almorzar mas temprano.
Say, rather, that you have been obliged to hunt the whole house for your books, as usual.	Di mejor que te fué menester buscar tus libros por toda la casa, como de costumbre.
If it is the breakfast that detained you, where is your excuse?	Si te detuvo el almuerzo endonde está tu escusa.
I have none, sir.	No tengo Señor.
Then you will remain an hour after school.	Entónces te quedaras una hora, despues de la escuela.
If it happens again, I will detain you Saturday afternoon.	Si te sucede otra vez, te detendré Sábado por la tarde.
Do you know your lesson?	Sabes tu leccion?
Come and say your lesson.	Ven acá; recita tu leccion.

---

* Endonde, where, in a place adonde, where, to a place

You do not know your lesson.	No sabes la leccion.
Study your lesson.	Estudia tu leccion.
You are doing nothing.	No haces nada.
Sir, I am studying my geography.	Señor estoy estudiando mi Geografia.
I told you to write your exercise.	Te he dicho que escribas tu tema.
Do your sums.	Haz tus sumas.
I must wash my slate.	Necesito lavar mi pizarra
Where is the sponge?	Endonde está la esponja?
I have no slate pencil.	No tengo lápiz.
Mr. B., will you give me a slate pencil, if you please.	Señor B. me hará V el favor de un lápiz.
Where is the one I gave you yesterday?	Endonde está él* que te dí ayer?
I have lost it.	Lo he perdido.
If you lose this, I shall punish you.	Si pierdes este, te castigaré.
Joseph, lend me your penknife.	José, préstame tu cortaplumas.
What to do?	Para hacer qué?
What do you want to do with it?	Que quiéres hacer con él.
I want to sharpen my slate pencil.	Quiero cortar mi lápiz.
I will not lend you my penknife to do that.	No te prestaré mi cortaplúmas para * hacer eso.
That will spoil it.	Eso le echa á perder.
A penknife is used to make pens with.	El cortaplumas se usa para cortar plumas.

---

* El distinguished from the article by the accent.

† Para is used to express *to* [before a verb,] when it means in order to, for the purpose of, &c.

I will lend you my knife.	Te prestaré mi cuchillo.
Do not shake the desk.	No (sacudas) menées la mesa de escribir.
You prevent me from writing.	No me dejas escribir.
Will you cease?	Estate quieto.
I will complain to Mr. B.	Me quejaré al Señor de B.
Do you know your lesson now?	Sabes tu leccion ahora?
Yes, sir, I believe I know it.	Sí Señor creo saberla.
Are you sure of it?	Estás seguro?
I have studied it as much as I could.	La he estudiado lo mas que pude.
Speak louder.	Habla mas alto.
You speak too low	Hablas demasiado bajo.
I cannot hear you.	No te puedo oir.
George, continue.	Jorje, adelante.
I have lost the place, sir.	Señor he perdido el lugar.
You were not attentive.	No estabas atento.
You shall copy a page after the school	Copiaras una pájina despues de la escuela.
How do you pronounce this word?	Como se pronuncia esta palabra?
William pronounce the same word.	Guillermo, pronúncia la misma palabra.
Take your copy-books.	Toma tus libros de copiar
I am going to give you pens.	Voy á darte plumas.*
Mr. B., I have no ink.	Señor de B., no tengo tinta.

---

* The plural of nouns is formed by adding *s* to those ending in a vowel and *es* if ending in a consonant.

The ink is too thick.	La tinta está demasiado es pesa.
The ink will not run.	No corre la tinta.
My pen is not good.	Mi pluma no es buena.
Bring it to me.	Traela acá.
I will make it.	La cortaré.
Lend me your penknife.	Prestame tu cortaplumas.
It does not cut.	No corta.
It is blunt	Está embotado.
You have spoiled it in cutting wood	V. lo ha echado á perder, cortando madera con él.
Will you have your pen hard or soft?	Quieres tu pluma dura ó blanda.
Hard, if you please.	Dura si V gusta.
Here it is.	Aquí está.
Try it.	Pruébala.
Are these pens made?	Estan cortadas estas plumas.
Make me that pen, if you please.	Hagame el favor de cortar esa pluma, si V. gusta.
This quill is bad.	Esta pluma es mala.
I will make a good pen of it.	Yo la haré buena.
How do you find it!	Está buena ahora?
It is a little too hard.	Está un poco dura.
Bring it here I will make it soft.	Traela acá y la dejaré mas blanda.
It is too fine.	Está demasiado fina.
It is not slit enough.	No da tinta bastante
It is excellent now.	Esta muy búena ahora.
I am very much obliged to you.	Muchas grácias.
Sit down properly.	Siéntate con propriedad.
Do not cross your legs	No cruces las piernas.

Do not put your feet on each other.	No pongas los piés sobre nadie.
Henry and Lewis, turn round towards me.	Henrique y Luis volvedme la cara.
You were talking together.	Estábais hablando juntos
No, Sir, I was studying my Latin grammar.	No Señor, estaba estudiando mi Gramática Latina.
Henry have you not spoken together.	Henrique no habeis estado juntos hablando?
Yes, Sir, Lewis told me something and I answered him.	Sí Señor, Luis me habló y le contesté.
Henry, did you not know it is ágainst the rules to speak during school.	Henrique, no sabias que era contra las reglas de la Escuela hablar en clase.
I had forgotten it.	Lo habia olvidado.
Well to make you remember it, I give you one page to copy after school.	Bueno, para hacertelo recordar, te doy una hoja que copiar despues de la clase.
And you Lewis, you shall copy one page for having spoken, and twelve pages, for having told a lie.	Y tú Luis copiaras una hoja por haber hablado y doce por haber dicho una mentira.
have told you often I will punish a lie twelve times more than any other fault.	Te he dicho muchas veces que te castigaria doce veces mas por una mentira que por otra falta cualquiera.
Where shall I sit?	En donde quiere V que me siente.

Where am I to sit.	En donde he de sentarme.
Sit by me.	Siéntate al lado de mí.
Sit on the chair.	Siéntate en esa silla
Sit further.	Siéntate mas allá.
Sit down on this bench.	Siéntate en este banco.
Go and sit down in your place.	Vete á sentar en tu lugar
Do not make any noise.	No hagas ruido.
Do not shake the table.	No menées la mesa.
Why do you shake the table.	Porqué menéas la mesa
Lend me your pen.	Préstame tu pluma.
Lend me your penknife.	Préstame tu cortaplumas.
Lend me your pencil.	Préstame tu lápiz.
I have lost my book.	He perdido mi libro.
I have lost my copy book.	He perdido mi libro de muestra.
Where did you leave it?	Endonde lo dejaste?
I left it on the table.	Lo dejé en la mesa
Here it is.	Aquí está.
I have found it.	Lo he encontrado.
Where was it?	En donde estaba?
It was under the bench.	Estaba debajo del banco.
Will you have the goodness to lend me your penknife?	Tengá V la bondad de prestarme su cortaplumas.
What do you want to do with it.	Que quiéres hacer con él?
I want to make a pen?	Quiero cortar una pluma
My pen is good for nothing	Mi pluma no vale nada.
I want to make it again.	Voy a cortarla otra vez.
It wants mending.	Necesita componerse.

GOING TO SCHOOL.

Why don't you use your penknife?	Porqué no te sirves de tu cortaplumas?
It does not cut at all	No corta nada.
It wants setting	Necesita afilarse.
I have entirely spoiled it in cutting my pencil	Lo he echado á perder cortando mi lápiz.
It is two o'clock	Son las dos.
I must go to school	Es necesário ir á la escuela
I am afraid to be too late	Temo que sea tarde.
You must come sooner another time	Ven mas temprano otra vez.
Do you know your lesson	Sabes tu leccion
Have you learned your lesson?	Has aprendido tu leccion?
What lesson have you learned?	Que leccion has aprendido?
You do not know your lesson	No sabes tu leccion.
You cannot say your lesson.	No puedes dar tu leccion.
Can you say your lesson now.	Puedes dar tu leccion?
I cannot say it perfectly.	No la sé perfectamente.
Why did you not learn your lesson?	Porqué no aprendiste tu leccion?
I forgot to learn it.	Me olvidé de aprenderla
Forgotten!!!	Olvidaste!!
This is a very bad excuse.	Mala escusa es esa.
I did not exactly forget it.	No puedo decir que la olvidé.
But we had company at our house last night.	Pero teníamos gente en casa á noche.
And I have not been able to study it.	Y no he podido estudiarla

If you had been diligent, you would have placed yourself in a corner and studied it.	Si hubieras tenido cuidado, te habrías puesto en algun rincon para estudiarla,
That is true.	Es verdad.
But I wanted to enjoy the company.	Pero queria gozar de la sociedad,
A good scholar should always have her task done before she sets about enjoying in any way.	El buen estudiante debe siempre aprender su leccion ántes de divertirse,
Having her task done, she will amuse herself with much more pleasure.	Acabada su leccion se divertirá con mucho mas gusto,

On the Spanish Language — Sobre la lengua Española

Do you speak Spanish?	Habla V Español?
I speak it a little.	Lo hablo un poco.
I speak it just enough to make myself understood.	Lo hablo* bastante para hacerme entender.
He speaks Spanish tolerably.	Habla el Español bastante bien.
Speak Spanish to me.	Hábleme V en Español
You pronounce well.	V pronuncia bien.
What book do you translate?	Que libro estás traduciendo?
I have translated P's Fables.	He traducido las Fábulas de P
Now I translate . .	Ahora estoy traduciendo,

---

*The third person singular of the perfect tense of the first conjunction, is the same as the first person of the indicative present being distinguished by the accent. Amo I love, amó, he loved.

What grammar do you use?	Por que gramática aprende V?
I first wrote the exercises of U's. grammar.	Al principio escribí los temas de la gramática de U.
I am now writing those of B's. grammar.	Ahora estoy escribiendo los de la gramática de B.
How long have you been learning Spanish?	Cuanto tiempo hace que está V aprendiendo el Español.
It is about a month.	Cerca de un mes.
You have improved much.	V ha adelantado mucho.
I would engage you to continue to apply yourself to it.	Aconsejo á V que continue aplicándose.
Spanish is spoken every where.	En todas partes se habla Español.
It is a language very much in use.	Es lengua que se usa mucho.
It is a language almost universal now.	Ahora es lengua casi universal.
English and Spanish, are the two most useful languages that one can learn.	El Yngles y el Español, son las dos lenguas mas útiles que se pueden aprender.
The English is in Europe, the language of well bred people.	El Yngles, en Europa es la lengua de la gente bien educada.
Do you intend learning English?	Piensa V en aprender el Yngles.
I am going to begin next month.	Voy á empezarlo el mes que viene.

I hope I shall go to England next year.	Espero ir á Ynglaterra el año próximo,
Then you will do well to learn English a little before you go.	Entónces hará V bien en aprender el Yngles, ántes de marcharse.
Apply yourself a little to grammar.	Estudie V un poco la gramática.
But above all commit to memory as great a number of phrases as you can.	Pero sobre todo aprenda V de memória el mayor número de frases que pueda.
In order to know a language thoroughly, grammar is absolutely necessary.	Para conocer perfectamente una lengua, la gramática es absolutamente necesaria.
In order to speak a language, you must learn phrases.	Para hablar una lengua, es preciso aprender frases.
One may be able to read and write a language and yet unable to speak.	Se puede leer y escribir una lengua, sin poder hablarla.
Written language differs much from the spoken language.	Hay una diferencia muy grande entre la lengua escrita y la lengua hablada.
Without the knowledge of the phrases, in conversation, one cannot express one's self.	Sin el conocimiento de algunas frases no puede uno esplicarse en una conversacion.

Of the Seasons. — De las Estaciones.

Winter is at last over.	Al fin, se acabó el Ynvierno.

OF THE SEASONS.

Do you like winter?	Le gusta á V el Ynvierno.
I like it as much as I do summer.	Me gusta tanto como el Verano.
You are perhaps the only one of this opinion	Acaso es V. solo de esa opinion.
In winter one is not comfortable, except by the fireside.	En Ynvierno no se puede estar, sino al lado del fuego.
Have you skated this winter?	Ha patinado V. este Ynvierno.
The winter has been very severe this year.	El Ynvierno ha sido muy riguroso este año.
I am glad to see the spring.	Me alegro que venga la Primavera.
It is the season I like best.	Es la estacion que mas me gusta.
It is the most pleasant of all seasons	Es la mas agradable de todas las estaciones.
The season is very backward.	La estacion está muy atrasada.
I fear we shall have a very hot summer.	Temo que tengamos un verano muy cálido.
One would think that the order of the seasons is inverted.	Se podria creer que se ha invertido el órden de las estaciones.
Summer is the season of the harvest.	El verano es la estacion de las cosechas.
It is also in this season that the grass is mowed.	Tambien en esta estacion se corta la yerba.
After Summer is autumn.	Despues del Verano viene el Otoño.

It is in autumn that the Vintages are made.	En Otoño se hace la Vendimia.
Towards the middle of autumn the mornings and evenings are cool.	Hácia el medio de Otoño, se ponen frescas las mañanas y las noches.
Then fire begins to be comfortable.	Entónces empieza á gustar el fuego.

Of the Weather. — Del Tiempo.

How is the weather?	Que tiempo hace?
What sort of weather is it?	Que tiempo es este?
Is it fine?	Hace buen tiempo?
Is it fine weather?	El tiempo está bueno?
Yes it is fine.	Sí hace buen tiempo.
The weather is settled.	Se ha asegurado el tiempo.
It is beautiful weather.	El tiempo está hermoso.
It is charming weather.	Hace un tiempo magnífico.
It is most delightful weather.	El tiempo está delicioso.
The weather is very close.	Hace un calor muy sofocante.
The weather is changeable.	El tiempo está variable.
The weather is unsettled	El tiempo está vario.
It gets cloudy.	Está poniéndose nublado
It is cloudy weather.	Está nebuloso.
It is bad weather.	Hace mal tiempo.
It is very bad weather.	Hace muy mal tiempo.
It is windy.	Hace viento.
It is very windy.	Hace mucho viento
The wind falls.	Calma el viento.

OF THE WEATHER.

It is foggy.	El tiempo está nebuloso
It is very foggy.	Está muy nebuloso.
The weather begins to clear up.	Se aclara el tiempo.
It is mild.	Está templado.
It is warm.	Hace calor.
It is cold.	Hace frio.
It is very hot.	Hace mucho calor.
It is very cold.	Hace mucho frio.
It is very sultry.	El dia está mui pesado.
It is dry weather	Hace un tiempo seco.
It is damp.	El tiempo está húmedo.
It threatens to rain	Amenaza llover.
It is going to rain.	Va á llover.
I feel drops of rain.	Siento gotas de llúvia.
It rains.	Llueve.
It rains very fast.	Llueve mucho.
It pours.	Llueve á torrentes.
It is pouring.	Está lloviendo a cántaros.
It is only a shower	Es una llovizna.
It does not rain.	No llueve.
The weather is stormy.	Hace un tiempo tempestuoso.
We shall have a storm.	Tendrémos tempestad.
Do you hear the thunder?	Oye V los truenos?
It thunders.	Está tronando.
The thunder roars	Los truenos bráman.
It lightens.	Relampaguea.
It has thundered and lightened all night.	Ha tronado y relampagueado toda la noche.
The weather clears up.	Se aclara el tiempo.
The weather settles.	El tiempo se asienta.
It freezes.	Está helando.
It freezes very hard	Hiela mucho

It freezes extremely hard.	Hiela fuertemente.
The river is frozen.	El rio está helado.
There is ice.	Hay hielo.
Is there ice?	Hay hielo?
The ice bears.	Se puede andar encima del hielo.
We shall have snow.	Tendrémos nieve.
It hails.	Graniza.
It is hailing.	Está granizando.
It is thawing.	Se está derritiendo la nieve.
It is dusty.	Hay polvo.
It snows.	Nieva.
It is snowing.	Está nevando.
There is much snow.	Hay mucha nieve.
I am very glad of it.	Me alegro mucho.
We shall go sleighing.	Vamos á pasear en trinéo.
Have you a sleigh.	Tiene V trineo.
It is good sleighing to-day.	Hoy está bueno para los trineos.
The rain has laid the dust.	La llúvia ha abatido el polvo.
The pavement is slipperry.	El suelo está resbaloso.
It is very bad walking.	Las calles estan malas.
It is day-light.	Amanece.
It is night.	Anochece.
It is dark.	Está obscuro.
It is very dark.	Está muy obscuro.
It is moon-light.	Está claro de luna.
The days are decreasing.	Los dias acórtan.
The days begin to decrease.	Comiénzan á acortar los dias.
The days are very short.	Los dias son muy cortos
I am warm.	Tengo calor.
I am cold.	Tengo frio.

Are you warm?	Tiene V calor?
Are you cold?	Tiene V frio?
Are you not warm?	No tiene V calor?
Are you not cold?	No tiene V frio?
I am quite wet.	Estoy mojado.
I am wet through.	Estoy empapado.
I am wet to the very skin	Estoy mojado hasta el pellejo.
Dry your clothes.	Seque V su ropa.
We shall have a fine day.	Tendrémos un dia hermoso.
The sun shines.	El sol está luciendo.
See what a beautiful rainbow.	Mire, que hermoso arco-íris.

Of Epochs. — De las Epocas.

Come to-day.	Venga V hoy.
Go there on Christmas.	Vaya V allá el dia de navidad.
It is broad-day-light.	Es dia claro.
The day you will come.	El dia que V venga.
The day will be fine.	Hará buen tiempo hoy.
I rise in the morning at six o'clock.	Me levanto á las seis de la mañana.
I have run the whole morning.	He corrido toda la mañana.
Send it to me this morning.	Envíemelo V esta mañana.
Come and spend your evening at my house.	Venga V á pasar la tarde conmigo.
I did it in the forenoon.	Lo hice ántes de mediodia
I will do it to-morrow morning.	Lo haré mañana por la mañana.

I shall go and see him the day after to-morrow.	Iré á verle pasado mañana.
I was there yesterday,	Estube ayer allá.
He sent it to me two days after.	Me lo envió dos dias despues.
The next day I went there.	Al dia siguiente fuí allá
The next day I saw him.	Le he visto el dia siguiente.
Two days ago.	Hace dos dias.
A fortnight ago.	Hace quince dias.
It is three weeks since.	Ya hace tres semanas.
Near about that time.	Cerca de ese tiempo.
Last month.	El mes pasado.
The year one thousand eight hundred and forty-nine.	El año de mil ocho cientos cuarenta y nueve.
Last year	El año pasado.
Next year.	El año que viene
Next year.	El año próximo venidero
I shall see you at Easter.	Le veré á V el dia de Pascua.
I shall move at mid-summer.	Me mudaré á mediados del verano.
At Michaelmas.	El dia de San Miguel.
The Indian summer.	El verano de los Indios,
The quarter is out.	Se cumplió el trimestre.
The next quarter.	El próximo trimestre.
The first of next month.	El primero del mes que viene.
The second of last month.	El dos del mes pasado,
The fourth of the present month.	El cuatro del mes presente.
The last day of the month.	El último del mes.
At the end of the month.	Al fin del mes.

OF EPOCHS.

Towards the middle of the month.	Hácia mediados del mes.
What day of the month is it?	A cuantos estamos del mes.
What day of the month is this?	A cuantos estamos hoy.
To-day is the fifteenth.	Hoy estamos á quince.
It is the first of the month.	Es el primero del mes.
No, it is the second.	No, estamos á dos.
I think it is the fifth.	Creo que estamos á cinco
In a fortnight.	En quince dias.
Next week.	La semana que viene.
Last week.	La semana pasada.
In a week.	En ocho dias.
This day week, (time to come.)	De hoy en ocho dias.
This day fortnight, (time to come.)	De hoy en quince dias.
This day week, (time past.)	Hoy hace ocho dias.
This day fortnight, (time past.)	Hoy hace quince dias.
It will soon be a week since.	Hace cerca de ocho dias.
We expect him from day to day.	Le estamos esperando todos los dias.
We shall go there one day or other.	Irémos allá algun dia.
I do it daily.	Lo hago todos los dias.
He says he will pay you one day or other.	Dice que le pagará algun dia.
Every day.	Todos los dias.
Every other day.	Cada dos dias.
He comes often.	Viene amenudo.
He is always speaking.	Está siempre hablando.

I seldom see him.	Le veo rara vez.
Never do that again.	No hagas mas eso.
A weekly paper.	Una gaceta semanal.
A daily paper.	Un diario.

Of the hour.   De la hora.

What o'clock is it?	Que hora es?
Tell me, if you please, what o'clock it is.	Hágame V el favor de decirme que hora es?
It is twelve o'clock.	Son las doce.
It is noon.	Es mediodia.
It is midnight.	Es media noche.
It is two o'clock.	Son las dos.
It is a quarter after two.	Son las dos y cuarto.
It is half past two.	Las las dos y media.
It is three quarters after two.	Son las dos y tres cuartos.
It wants a quarter to three.	Falta un cuarto para las tres.
It is very near four.	Son cerca de las cuatro
It has just struck five.	Acaban de dar las cinco.
It is twenty minutes after five o'clock.	Son las cinco y veinte minutos.
It wants twenty-five minutes to six o'clock.	Son las seis ménos veinte y cinco.
Does your watch go well?	Anda bien su relox de V.
My watch does not go well.	Mi relóx no va bien.
My watch goes too fast.	Mi relóx adelanta.
It goes too slow,	Atrasa.
It gains a quarter of an hour every day.	Adelanta un cuarto cada veinte y cuatro horas

It loses half an hour every day.	Atrasa media hora cada veinte y cuatro.
It stops now and then.	Se para de cuando en cuando.
My watch is right.	Mi relox anda bien.
It is not right.	No anda bien.
It is too fast.	Adelanta.
It is too slow.	Atrasa.
It is early.	Es temprano.
It is late.	Es tarde.
It is very late.	Es muy tarde.
Come about seven o'clock.	Venga á eso de las siete
Do you know what o'clock it is?	Sabe que hora es?
I don't know.	No lo sé.
I cannot tell you exactly.	No le puedo decir ecsactamente.
Look at your watch.	Mire su relóx.
It is not wound up.	No le he dado cuerda.
I forgot to wind it up.	Olvidé darle cuerda.
It does not go.	Está parado.
It has stopped.	Se ha parado.
What o'clock is it by yours.	Que hora tiene V.
Does yours go well?	Anda bien su reló de V
Mine does not go well.	No va bien el mio.
It is not right.	No anda bien.
It is out of order.	Está desarreglado.
Something is out of order in it.	Tiene alguna cosa descompuesta.
Smething is broken in it	Se ha roto algo.
The main spring is broken.	Se há roto el muelle real

I think the chain is broken.	Creo que se rompió la cadena.
Have it mended.	Mándele V. componer.
I am going to send it to the Watchmaker.	Voy á mandarlo al relojero.
You will do well.	Hará V. bien.
Send it to Mr. A...	Mandelo á casa de
He is a good watchmaker.	Es buen relojero. *
Yes but he charges very high.	Sí, pero pide muy caro.
That's true, but one may rely on what he does.	Es verdad, pero se puede depender de lo que hace.
My watch is a French watch.	Mi reló es Frances.
I bought it at Paris.	Lo compré en Paris.
My watch is a repeater.	Mi reló és de repeticion.

News. — Noticias.

Is there any news to-day?	Hay noticias hoy?
Is there anything new?	Hay algo de nuevo?*
Do you know anything new?	Sabe V. algo de nuevo?
Do you know any news?	Sabe V algunas noticias.
What is the news?	Que noticias hay?
What news is there?	Que hay de nuevo?
What news can you tell us?	Que dice V. de nuevo?
Have you got any thing to tell us?	Tiene V. algo que decirnos.

---

* In speaking of trades. professions, &c. the singular is not used carpintero, ne is a carpenter. Soy medico, I am a doctor, &c.
† Any thing good, algo de bueno. &c.

NEWS.

Have you not heard of any thing?	No ha oido V. decir nada?
What is the talk about town?	Que se dice por la villa?
What is the news in your quarter?	Que noticias hay por ahí.
I know nothing new.	No sé nade de nuevo.
There is no news.	No hay noticia ninguna.
I know no news.	No sé noticia ninguna.
I have not heard of any thing.	No he oido nada.
There is no talk of any thing.	No se dice nade de nuevo.
There are good news.	Hay buenas noticias.
The news is good.	Las noticias son buenas.
There are bad news.	Hay malas noticias.
The news are very bad.	Las noticias son malas.
That is good news.	Son buenas noticias.
That is bad news.	Esa es mala noticia.
I have heard that. . . .	He oido decir que.
I did not hear of that.	No he oido eso.
Did you read the papers?	Ha leido V. los diários?
What do the papers say?	Que dicen los diários.
I have read no paper to-day.	No he leido hoy la gazeta?
Did you see that in any paper?	Vió V eso en la gazeta?
It is only mentioned in a private letter.	Se dice solamente en carta privada.
Do they say who received that letter?	Dicen quien recibió esa carta?
They doubt this news much.	Esta noticia se duda mucho.
This news wants confirmation.	Esa noticia necesita confirmacion.

From whom have you had that news?	De quien ha recibido V. esa noticia?
How do you know that?	Como sabe V. eso?
I have that news from good authority.	Recibí esa noticia de buena autoridad.
That news has not been confirmed.	No ha sido confirmada esa noticia.
That report has proved false.	Aquella noticia ha salido falsa.
That is no longer talked of.	No se habla mas de eso.
Do they still talk of war?	Se habla todavía de guerra?
Do they think we shall have peace?	Se cree que tendrémos paz?
It is not likely.	No es probable.
Have you heard from your brother?	Ha recibido V. carta de su hermano?
Did you hear lately from your friend.	Recibió V. ultimamente noticia de su amigo?
How long is it since he wrote to you?	Hace mucho que le escribió á V?
I have not heard from him these two months.	Hace dos meses que no he recibido carta suya.
He has not written for these three weeks.	Hace tres semanas que no me escribió.
I expect from Paris a letter from him every day.	Estoy esperando carta de él, todos los dias de Paris.
What does he say to you about Paris?	Que le dice á V. de Paris?
He gives me a description of most of the curiosities of that City.	Me da una descripcion de casi todas las curiosidades de esa ciudad.

Is he pleased with Paris?	Le gusta Paris ?
He amuses himself so much there, that he does not speak of returning.	Se divierte tanto allí, que no dice nada de volver.

Of the Age. — De la Edad.

How old are you ?	Cuantos años tiene V ?
What is your age ?	Cuantos años tiene ?
What may be his age ?	Que edad puede tener ?
How old may he be ?	Que edad tendrá ?
He will be twelve the fifteenth of next month.	Cumplirá doce años el quince del mes que viene.
I shall soon be ten.	Luego tendré diez años.
I am twenty five.	Tengo veinte y cinco años.
How old is your father ?	Que edad tiene su padre de V ?
What is your brother's age ?	Cuantos años tiene su hermano ?
How old is your brother ?	Que edad tiene su hermano de V ?
He is not yet twenty.	Todavia no tiene veinte años.
He is not yet of age.	Aun no es mayor de edad.
He is still under age.	Es todavía menor.
How old may that child be ?	Que edad puede tener ese niño ?
He is only six years old.	Tiene solamente seis años.
He is tall for his age ?	Es grande para su edad.
How old is your sister ?	Que edad tiene su hermana ?
She is more than seven.	Tiene mas de siete años

She is almost eight.	Tiene cerca de ocho años.
She is twenty.	Tiene veinte años.
She is in her bloom.	Está en la flor de su edad.
Your uncle must be very near forty years old.	Su tio debe* de tener cerca de cuarenta años
He is in his forty-second year.	Tiene cuarenta y dos años.
He is in the prime of life, your grandmother appears very aged.	Está en la flor de su edad; su abuela de V parece muy vieja.
How old do you think she is?	Cuantos años le parece á V que tiene?
She cannot be more than eighty.	No puede tener mas de ochenta años?
She is eighty-four.	Tiene ochenta y cuatro.
We keep every year her birth day.	Celebramos sus dias todos los años.
She is older than I.	Tiene mas años que yo.
I did not think her so old.	No la creia tan vieja.
She carries her age well.	Tiene buena vejez.
Her father is still living.	Vive todavía su padre.
He must be very old.	Debe ser muy viejo.
He is just entering into his hundreth.	Le falta poco para cien años.
He has become quite childish.	Se ha vuelto niño.

Morning.   De la Mañana

You are up?	Está V levantado?

* When "must" does not imply absolute necessity "deber" own is used.

You are up already.	Está V ya levantado.
I have been up this hour.	Hace una hora que me levanté.
You got up very early.	V se levantó muy temprano.
I commonly rise early.	Tengo costumbre de levantarme temprano.
It is a very good habit.	Es muy buena costumbre.
It is very good for the health.	Es muy bueno para la salud.
How did you sleep last night.	Como pasó V la noche?
I never awoke all night.	No me desperté en toda la noche.
I slept without waking.	Dormí sin despertarme una sola vez.
And you, how did you rest?	Y V, como pasó la noche?
Not very well.	No muy bien.
I did not sleep very well.	No dormí muy bien.
I could not sleep.	No podia dormir.
I never closed my eyes once last night.	No cerré los ojos en toda la noche.
This is a fine morning.	Hace una mañana hermosa.
What do you think of taking a little walk?	Que le parece V de un paseito.
Shall we have time before breakfast?	Tendremos tiempo ántes de almorzar?
We have plenty of time, they will not breakfast this hour.	Tenemos bastante tiempo; no almorzaran hasta de aquí á una hora.

We have full an hour before us.	Tenemos todavia una buena hora.
Well, let us go for a little airing.	Bueno, vámos á tomar un poco el ayre.
It will sharpen our appetite.	Nos dará apetito.

Of the necessaries of life. — De las cosas necesárias á la vida.

I am hungry.	Tengo hambre.
I am very hungry.	Tengo mucha hambre.
I am dying with hunger.	Me muero de hambre.
I feel an appetite.	Me siento con apetito
I am thirsty.	Tengo sed.
I am dying with thirst.	Me muero de sed.
I could drink with pleasure.	Bebería con gusto.
Give me some thing to drink.	Deme algo que beber.
Give me a glass of water.	Deme un vaso de agua.
I am very tired.	Estoy muy cansado.
I am very much fatigued.	Estoy muy fatigado.
I am exhausted with fatigue.	Estoy ecsausto de fatiga
I am cold.	Tengo frio
My hands are cold	Tengo las manos frias.
I am warm.	Tengo calor.
I am quite sleepy.	Tengo sueño.
I feel quite drowsy.	Tengo mucho sueño.
I think I shall sleep well.	Creo que dormiré bien
I am overcome with sleep.	Me estoy cayendo de sueño

I wish I was in bed.	Quisiera estar en la cama.
I have slept well.	He dormido bien.
I could not get to sleep.	No podia dormir.
I have not been able to close my eyes once all night.	No he cerrado los ojos en toda la noche.

Fire / Fuego.

Here is a poor fire.	El fuego está malo.
Here is a very bad fire.	Hay muy mal fuego.
You have not taken care of the fire.	V. no ha cuidado del fuego.
You have not kept the fire up.	V no ha sostenido el fuego.
You have let the fire go down.	V ha dejado amortiguar el fuego.
You have let the fire out.	V ha dejado apagarse el fuego.
It is not quite out.	No se apagó enteramente
It must be lighted up again.	Es preciso encenderlo otra vez.
Come and make up the fire.	Venga V á encender de nuevo la candela.
What do you look for?	Que está V buscando?
I am looking for the tongs.	Estoy buscando las tenazas.
Here they are in the corner.	Aquí están en la esquina
Where are the bellows?	Endonde está el fuelle?
Blow the fire.	Sople el fuego.
Go and fetch the bellows.	Vete á buscar el fuelle

Blow it gently.	Sopla un poco el fuego.
Do not blow so hard.	No sople tan fuerte.
Put a few shavings under.	Ponga algunas raeduras abajo.
Now put on two or three pieces of wood.	Ahora ponga algunos pedazos de leña.
The fire will soon draw up.	Se encenderá pronto
Is there any coal in the scuttle?	Hay carbon en la banasta?
Take the shovel and put some coal on the fire.	Tome la pala y ponga carbon en el fuego.
Do not put too much at a time.	No ponga V. demasiado á la vez.
If you put too much, you will put the fire out.	Si V pone demasiado, apagará el fuego.
You have almost smothered the fire.	V ha casi apagado el fuego.
Raise it up with the poker.	Levántelo V con el hurgon.
It will give it a little air.	Eso le dará un poco de ayre.
The fire begins to blaze.	El fuego ya flambea.
Now this fire is very good.	Ahora está bueno el fuego.
You have made it up again very well.	V lo ha compuesto perfectamente.
Which do you prefer a coal fire, or a wood fire?	Cual le gusta á V mas el fuego de carbon de piedra, ó él de carbon de leña?
I prefer a wood fire.	Prefiero el fuego de leña.

FIRE.

As for me I prefer a coal fire.	Yo prefiero el fuego de carbon.
A wood fire does not give so much heat.	Fuego de leña no da tanto calor.
And it gives much trouble to keep it up.	Y da mucho trabajo e, conservarlo.
A coal fire, made up in the morning, lasts almost the whole day long.	El fuego de carbon hecho por la mañana dura casi todo el dia.
Do you burn your coal in a grate?	Enciende V el fuego en las parrillas.
No, in a stove.	No, en la estufa.
I do not like stoves.	No me gustan las estufas.
I like to see the blaze.	Me gusta ver la llama.

Going to Market. — De ir á la Plaza.

I must go to market.	Es preciso que vaya á la plaza.
I shall buy some chickens.	Compraré pollos.
Perhaps a pair of ducks.	Puedeser un par de patos.
Here is a couple of nice ducks.	Aquí hay un par de patos buenos.
Have you fresh eggs?	Tiene huevos frescos?
How many pounds of butter do you want?	Cuantas libras de mantequilla quiere V?
I forgot something at home.	He olvidado algo en casa.
I must go back.	Necesito volver
Mary you will finish marketing.	Maria, tu acabarás las compras.

Take three pounds of butter, if it is good.	Tome tres libras de mantequilla, si es buena.
As you come back call at the butcher's.	A la vuelta pase á casa del carnicero
What meat shall I order?	Que carne quiere V que mande?
Let him send a sirloin for to-day.	Que mande un lomo para hoy.
For to-morrow two or three ribs of beef.	Para mañana dos ó tres costillas de vaca.
And for the day after a leg of mutton.	Y para pasado mañana una pierna de carnero.
I should like to have a breast of veal.	Me gustaria un pecho de ternera.
If there is none to be got, take a loin of veal.	Si no hay, tome un lomo de ternera.
Do not forget a quarter of lamb.	No olvide un cuarto de cordero.
A shoulder of mutton.	Una pierna de adelante del carnero.
A calf's head.	Cabeza de ternera.
A neck of mutton	Pescuezo de carnero.
Ask him whether he has a good sweet bread.	Pregúntele si tiene una buena molleja.
If he has none, get it somewhere else.	Si no tiene, búsquela en otra parte.
See whether he has got a nice beef's tongue.	Vea si tiene buena lengua de vaca.
Let him send all this directly.	Que lo mande todo al instante.
Tell him to send the bill with it.	Dígale que mande tambien la cuenta.
Do you wish me to buy fish.	Quiere V que compre pescado.

Yes I forgot to mention it.	Sí, olvidé decírselo.*
Is there any fish in the market.	Hay pescado en la plaza?
There is plenty of fish.	Hay bastante pescado.
There is hardly any fish.	Hay muy poco pescado.
What sort of fish are those?	Que clase de pescado es ese?
They are herrings and mackerel.	Son sardinas y escombros.
Buy a shad.	Compre una alosa.
Will you have a salmon?	Quiere V un salmon.
I prefer a fresh cod.	Prefiero el bacalao fresco.
I have seen a fine turbot.	He visto un rombo hermoso.
How much do soles sell for?	A como venden los lenguados?
They sell according to the size.	Se venden segun el tamaño.
A couple of pretty nice ones may be sold for a dollar.	Se puede vender un par, bastante grandes por un duro.
Is there any shell-fish.	Hay algun marisco.
Are we in the season for shell-fish.	Es el tiempo de marisco.
There are to be had crabs and lobsters.	Se puede lograr cangrejos y langostas.
Buy a few of them.	Compre algunas.

Breakfast. — Almuerzo.

Have you breakfasted?	Ha almorzado V?

---

* Both pronouns the objects of the infinitive or imperative-affirmative, must be joined to it, as one word

Not yet.	Todavia no.
You come just in time.	Viene V. á tiempo.
You will breakfast with us?	Almorzará V. con nosotros.
Is breakfast ready?	Está listo el almuerzo?
It will soon be ready.	Pronto estará listo.
Breakfast is ready.	El almuerzo está listo.
Come, Madam.	Venga V. Señora.
Everybody is in the parlour.	Todos estan en la sala.
They only wait for you.	No esperan mas que á V
I am coming down directly.	Bajo al instante.
I beg your pardon for having kept you waiting.	Perdone V. el haberle hecho esperar.
Do you drink tea or coffee.	Toma V. té ó café?
Here is coffee.	Aquí hay café.
There is tea.	Allí hay té.
You have near you chocolate.	Tiene V. el chocolate cerca de V.
Which do you prefer?	Cual prefiere V?
Which do you like best.	Cual le gusta á V mas?
I prefer coffee.	Prefiero el café.
I will thank you for some chocolate.	Hágame V. el favor de darme chocolate.
Is your coffee sweet enough.	Tiene V. bastante azúcar?
It is excellent and very clear.	Es escelente y muy claro
Here are rolls.	Aquí hay pan fresco.
There is toast.	Allí hay tostada.
I shall take a roll.	Tomaré pan fresco.
I prefer some toast.	Prefiero tostada.

Do me the kindness to pass the butter	Hágame V. el favor de pasarme la mantequilla.
Give me the bread if you please?	Hágame V. el favor del pan.
The tea is rather weak.	El té está flojo.
I like it strong.	Me gusta fuerte.
I drink it without sugar.	Yo lo bebo sin azúcar.
What shall I offer you?	Que le ofreceré á V?
Nothing more I thank you.	Nada mas, gracias.
Do you take cream with your coffee.	Toma V nata en su café?
Here are some fresh eggs allow me to send you one.	Aquí hay huevos frescos, permítame V que le dé algunos.
Will you have a bit of cold meat?	Quiere V. un poco de carne fria?
Will you have a sausage?	Quiere V. salchichon?
I have made an excellent breakfast.	He almorzado muy bien.
I can now wait for dinner very well.	Ahora puedo muy bien esperar la comida.

Dinner.   La Comida.

It will soon be two o'clock.	Luego serán las dos.
It is almost two o'clock.	Son cerca de las dos.
It is nearly two o'clock.	Falta poco para las dos.
It is very near two o'clock	Falta muy poco para las dos.
Let us return home.	Volvamos á casa.
What time do we dine at to-day?	A que hora se come hoy.
The cloth will be laid presently.	Se pondrá la mesa luego.

Dinner is on the table.	La comida está en la mesa
Let us sit down.	Sentémonos*.
Let us place ourselves at table.	Arrimémonos á la mesa.
No not yet.	No, todavía no.
Do you expect company?	Espera V gente.
I expect Mr. and Mrs. B...	Espero al Sénor y á la Sénora de B...
Have you given orders for dinner?	Ha mandado V traher la comida?
What have you ordered?	Que ha mandado?
What shall we have for dinner?	Que tendrémos para comer?
Shall we have any fish?	Tendrémos pescado?
There was no fish in the market.	No habia pescado en la plaza.
Mr. and Mrs. B. will not come.	El Señor y la Señora B... no vendran.
Let us begin dinner.	Empezemos la comida.
What shall I offer you?	Que gusta V?
Will you have some soup?	Quiere V sopa?
Will you take some soup?	Quiere V tomar sopa?
I thank you.	Gracias.
I will trouble you for a little beef.	Hágame el favor de un poco de carne.
It looks very nice.	Parece muy buena.
This fowl is delicious.	Este pollo está delicioso.
Will you have a wing?	Quiere V una ala?
If you please.	Si V gusta.
I will thank you for some gravy.	Me hace V el favor de un poco salsa.
Shall I give you some vegetables?	Gusta V legumbres.

The final s in the verb is omitted here for the sake of euphony

A potato if you please.	Una papa, si V quiere.
Will you have a little sauce?	Serviré á V un poco de salsa.
Shall I offer you a piece of this roast beef?	Le daré á V. un pedacito de esta carne asada.
will willingly take a small piece.	Tomaré un poco con gusto.
Will you have it well done.	Lo quiere vd. bien cocido?
Will you have it underdone?	Lo quiere V. un poco crudo?
Rather well done.	Lo prefiero bien cocido?
Rather rare.	Un poco crudo.
Did I help you to your liking?	Le he dado á V lo que le gusta?
It is excellent.	Es escelente.
It is as tender as chicken.	Es tierno como un pollo.
Gentlemen, give me leave to drink your health.	Señores, permítanme ustedes que beba á su salud.
I will take some salad.	Tomare ensalada.
This claret is delicious.	Este vino de Burdéos es delicioso.
Let us have a bottle of champaign.	Tomemos una botella de Champaña.
How do you like it?	Le gusta á V?
It is very agreeable to the taste.	Es muy agradable al paladar.
Have you any good cheese?	Tiene V buen queso?
Bring some.	Traiga un poco.
Bring the desert.	Traiga los postres.
We have had a good dinner.	Hemos comido bien.

† Ito is added to nouns to express diminutiveness, also as a term of affection. Ito added, makes a thing small and pretty; uelo, small and ugly.

Let us taste these peaches.	Probemos esos melocotones.
These pears are delicious.	Estas peras son deliciosas.
Give me a bit of cheese.	Deme un pedacito de queso.
Which will you have, ?	De cual quiere V ?
English cheese.	Del queso Ingles,
You give me too much.	V me pone demasiado.
There is but a mouthful.	No hay mas que un bocado.
Give me but the half of it.	Deme solamente la mitad
Cut that in two.	Corte eso en dos.
You may clear the table.	Puede quitar la mesa.
Bring us some wine.	Traiga vino.
Dinner is over.	Se acabó la comida.

Tea. — El Té.

It is seven o'clock.	Son las siete,
Tea will be ready in a moment	Luego estará listo el te.
Do you hear the bell ?	Oye V la campana. ?
Let us go down.	Vamos abajo.
Sit down, gentlemen.	Siéntense ustedes Señores
I like tea without sugar.	Me gusta el té sin azúcar,
And I without cream	Y á mí sin nata,
I like tea strong.	Me gusta el té fuerte.
Allow me to give you another cup.	Permítame V servirle otra taza,
I never take more than one cup.	Nunca tomo mas que una taza,
Now in France people drink a good deal of tea.	Ahora en Francia se bebe mucho té,
The English have introduced the use of it.	Los Ingleses lo han introducido.

Bring some more boiling water,	Traiga mas agua caliente.
This water is not warm enough.	Esta agua no esta bastante caliente.
There is fresh butter.	Aquí hay manteca fresca.
This is good bread.	Este pan es bueno.
I will willingly take half a cup more.	Tomaré con gusto otra media taza.
I shall go and take tea tomorrow at your house.	Mañana iré á tomar el té en su casa de V.
I shall be very glad to see you.	Me alegraré mucho verle á V.
We take tea exactly at seven.	Tomamos el té á las siete en punto.
I shall let you taste excellent green tea.	Le haré probar té verde escelente.
I prefer black.	Prefiero el negro.

Supper. — La Cena.

Will you stay and sup with us,	Quiere V quedarse á cenar con nosotros.
Sup with us without ceremony.	Cene V con nosotros sin ceremonia.
Bring a plate, a knife and a fork for this gentleman.	Traiga un plato, y cubierto para este Señor.
No, truly.	No, de veras.
I never take any supper.	Nunca ceno.
Well, sit near the table.	Bueno acérquese V á la mesa.
We will talk.	Hablarémos.
You will take a glass of wine.	V tomará un vaso de vino.

You cannot refuse that.	Eso no puede V. rehusar
Do you like oysters?	Le gustan á V ostras?
I am very fond of them.	Me gustan mucho.
I will eat a few.	Tomaré algunas.
How do you find them?	Le gustan á V?
They are good, and very fresh.	Son buenas y muy frescas.
Will you take a slice of cold turkey?	Quiere V tomar un poco de este pavo frio?
No, I thank you.	No, gracias.
I am satisfied with my piece of bread and butter.	Estoy contento con mi pedacito de pan y queso.
Will you take a glass of beer?	Quiere V tomar un vaso de cerveza.
Willingly, I do not like tea.	De buena gana; no me gusta el té.
In England the beer is excellent.	En Inglaterra la cerveza es escelente.
I like small beer.	Me gusta la pequeña cerveza.
It is an agreeable and wholesome drink.	Es una bebida agradable y sana.

Going to bed.

De ir á la cama.

Let us see the room I am to sleep in.	Déjeme ver el cuarto en donde voy á dormir.
Will you show me to my bed-room?	Me enseñará V mi cuarto?
I should like a room on the first floor.	Me gustaria cuarto en el primer piso.
Give me a retired and quiet apartment.	Deme un cuarto retirado y tranquilo.

GOING TO BED.

Your room is quite ready.	Su cuarto de V está listo.
Well, show me the way, I will follow you.	Bueno, enséñeme el camino, yo le seguiré.
Nobody lodges above you.	Nádie aloja en el cuarto de arriba.
Shut the window shutters.	Cierre los postigos.
Bring up my baggage in my room.	Lleve las maletas á mi cuarto.
Where have you put our things?	En donde ha puesto V nuestro equipage.
Are the beds well aired?	Están ventiladas las camas?
These sheets feel damp.	Me parecen húmedas estas sábanas.
I must have others.	Quiero otras.
Warm my bed.	Caliente mi cama.
It is very cold.	Hace mucho frio.
I shall want another blanket.	Necesitaré otra frazada.
This is too light.	Esta es demasiado lijera.
Give me another pillow.	Deme otra almohada.
Put some water in my basin.	Ponga agua en mi jarro.
Will you have a night lamp?	Quiere V bujia.
No, that would prevent my sleeping.	No, me impediria dormir.
Take away the candle.	Lleve la vela.
I will put it out myself.	Yo la apagaré.
Before you go, draw the curtains.	Ántes que se vaya baje las cortinas.
Is there a bell in this room?	Hay campanilla en este cuarto?

GOING TO BED.

At what time do you wish to get up to morrow?	A que hora quiere V levantarse mañana?
When am I to call you?	Cuando quiere V que se le llame.
Exactly at six.	A las seis en punto.
I must set off early.	Tengo que marcharme temprano.
I will not fail to come and awake you.	No dejaré de venir á dispertarle.
You may rely upon me.	V. puede depender de mí.
I wish to have my bill.	Quiero mi cuenta.
Is it ready?	Está hecha?
Tell your master to send me his bill.	Diga á su amo que me mande mi cuenta.
I will settle with him to-night.	Arreglaré con él esta noche.
What have I to pay?	Cuanto hay que pagar?
What is my expense?	Cuanto es el gasto?
I have brought your bill.	Le he traido á V su cuenta.
It amounts to ten dollars.	Sube á diez pesos.
It is very high.	Es muy subida.
Here is your money.	Aquí está su dinero.
It is all right.	Todo está completo.
This bill is reasonable.	La cuenta es regular.
Now I must sleep.	Ahora necesito dormir.
Does the door shut well?	Cierra bien la puerta?
Where is the key?	Endonde está la llave?
Is there a bolt?	Hay cerrojo?
Sir, I wish you a good night's rest.	Señor, que V pase buena noche.
This bed is very hard.	Esta cama está muy dura

I think I shall not be able to sleep.	No creo que pueda dormir.
There is only one mattress	No hay mas que un jergon.
Let us try to sleep.	A ver si podémos dormir.

Inquiries relative to a Journey.	Preguntas de un Viage
I want to go to . . .	Quiero ir á . .
Is the road good?	Está bueno el camino.
It is not very bad.	No está muy malo.
It is shocking in winter.	En Ynvierno es malísimo.
It is pretty good in this season.	En esta estacion está bastante bueno.
Is the road sandy?	El camino es arenoso?
The road is broad.	El camino es ancho.
I am going to take my seat at the coach office.	Voy á tomar mi asiento en el paradero de la diligencia.
I prefer going by the mail.	Prefiero ir con el correo.
I do not like the steamboat.	No me gustan los barcos de vapor.
How much is my fare?	Cuanto es lo que se paga?
Three dollars and six cents.	Tres pesos y seis centavos.
How many miles are there from here to B. * * *?	Cuantas millas hay de aquí á B, * *
I did not think it was so far.	No lo creia tan léjos.

When shall we start?	Cuando marcharémos?
To-morrow at six o'clock.	Mañana á las seis de la mañana.
And at what o'clock shall we reach B. * *?	Y á que hora llegarémos á B?
At eight in the evening.	A las ocho de la noche
Where are we to breakfast?	Endonde almorzámos?
Where shall we dine?	Endonde comerémos?
Where shall we drink tea?	Endonde tomarémos el té?
All the passengers are here.	Todos los pasageros están aquí.
Let us start then.	Pues, vamos.
Driver, what keeps you from starting?	Cochero, que le impide á V ponerse en camino?
At last we have started.	Al fin, estamos en camino
Shut the door.	Cierre la puerta
Where are we?	Endonde estamos?
What is the name of this village?	Como se llama este pueblo?
Does the coach stop here?	Para aquí el coche?
Yes, sir, to change horses.	Sí Señor, para cambiar el tiro.
Shall we have time to take any thing?	Tendrémos tiempo para tomar algo?
What hotel does the coach put up at?	En que Hotel se para el coche?
At the United States Hotel, in Fulton Street.	En el Hotel de los Estados Unidos, en la calle de Fulton.
We are at last arrived.	Al fin, hemos llegado
Is one comfortable there?	Estará uno bien ahí?
Quite so.	Perfectamente

Sir. have you any baggage to carry?	Señor, tiene V algunos baules que llevar?
Yes, take this trunk	Sí, lleve esta maleta.
Yes, take this portmanteau.	Sí, toma este baul.
I want a room with a single bed.	Necesito un cuarto con una cama sola.
At what o'clock do we sup?	A que hora se cena?
At half past eight.	A las ocho y media.
I shall go to bed early.	Me acostaré temprano.
I am very tired.	Estoy muy cansado.
The road was so bad.	El camino estaba muy malo.
Why did you not choose the steamboat?	Porqué no tomó el Vapor.
One travels by it much more comfortably.	Se viaja mucho mas agradable.
I think another time I shall take it.	Creo que lo tomaré otra vez.

Parting — De despedirse.

I must go away	Es preciso que me vaya.
I must leave you.	Me es menester dejarle.
We must part.	Hemos de separarnos.
I must take my leave of you.	Es preciso que me despida de V.
I am going to take my leave of you.	Voy á decirle á V adios.
Till I have the honor of seeing you again.	Hasta tener el gusto de volver á verle á V.
Good bye.	Adios.
Till we meet again.	Hasta otra vez.

To our next meeting.	Hasta cada rato.
To our next meeting.	Hasta la primera vista.
Your servant, sir.	Servidor de V Señor.
Your servant, madam.	Servidor de V Señora.
Your humble servant.	A los pies de V.
I wish you good morning.	Tenga V buenos dias.
I wish you good evening.	Tenga V buenas tardes.
I wish you good night.	Tenga buenas noches.
My compliments to your brother.	Memorias á su hermano.
Give my regards to your sister.	Muchas memórias á su hermana.
Present my respects to your mother.	Presento V mis respetos á su madre.
Present my duty to your aunt.	Pongame V a los pies de su tia.
Give my kind regards to your lady.	Muchas memorias de mi parte á su señora.
Remember me to all at home.	Memorias á todos de casa.
I will not fail.	No dejaré de hacerlo.

Inquiring one's way. — Para informarse del camino.

Is this the way to . . ?	Es este el camino de ?
Is this the way to go to . . ?	Es este el camino para ?
Is this the way that leads to . . ?	Se va por aquí para ?
Does this way lead to . . ?	Se va por este camino á ?
You are in the right way.	V va bien.
You are in the wrong way.	V va mal.

How far is it from here to . . ?	Cuanto hay de aquí á . . ?
Is it far from here to . . ?	Es léjos de aquí.
Is it very far from here to . ?	Es muy léjos de aquí á. ?
No, it is not far.	No, no es léjos.
It is hardly two miles.	Hay escasamente dos millas.
It is only two steps from here.	Está á dos pasos de aquí?
It is only a short league.	No hay mas que una legua corta.
One French league.	Una legua francesa.
One English mile.	Una milla Ynglesa.
Three miles are one league	Tres millas hacen una legua.
It is about one mile.	Hay cerca de una milla.
It is full a mile from here to . . ?	Hay una buena milla de aquí á. . . .
It is full a mile.	Hay una milla buena.
Which way am I to go?	Por que camino iré?
Which way must I go?	Por donde es preciso que vaya?
Which way must I go?	Por donde debo ir?
Go straight on.	Vaya V derecho.
Go to the right.	Vaya por la derecha.
Go to the left.	Tome V á la izquierda.
You will turn to the right at the first corner, then to the left, and then keep straight on.	En la primera esquina tomará V á la derecha, luego a la izquierda y despues siga V derecho.

To inquire for the residence of a person.	Para informarse de la residencia de una persona.
Will you have the goodness to tell me . . . ?	Tendrá V la bondad de decirme?
Will you tell me if you please . . . ?	Me hará el favor de decirme?
Where does Mr. B. live?	Endonde vive el señor B.?
Do you know Mr. B.?	Conoce V al señor B.?
No, sir.	No, señor.
No, sir, I do not.	No, señor, no le conozco.
I do not know any body of that name here.	No conozco á nadie, de ese nombre aquí.
Yes, sir, I know him.	Sí señor, le conozco.
I know him very well.	Le conozco muy bien.
I have the honour of knowing him.	Tengo el honor de conocerle.
Will you favour me with his address.	Me hará V el favor de dirigirme á su casa?
In what street does he live?	En que calle vive?
He lives in Bond Street.	Vive en la calle Bond.
Is it far from here?	Está léjos de aquí?
It is but two steps off.	Está muy cerca.
Can you direct me to his house?	Puede V dirigirme á su casa.
I am going that way myself.	Voy por ese camino.
I will show you his house.	Le enseñaré su casa.
It is very far from here.	Está léjos de aquí.
In that case I will take a hackney coach.	En ese caso tomaré coche de alquiler.
Call for a coach.	Mande V un coche.

MEETING A FRIEND.

Coachman drive me in Fifth Street, number four.	Cochero, condúzcame V á la calle quinta número cuatro.
Stop at this house.	Párese en esta casa.
On the right side going up.	Subiendo, á la derecha.
On the left side going down.	Bajando, á la izquierda.
At that brick house.	En esa casa de ladrillos.
At that marble house.	En esa casa de mármol.

Meeting a Friend.
Al encontrar un amigo,

What! is it you?	Que! es V?
Is it really you?	De véras es V?
No other.	No es otro.
It is I personally.	Yo mismo.
You quite surprise me.	V me sorprende mucho.
I did not expect to meet you here.	No esperaba encontrarle á V aquí.
I am very happy to see you.	Me alegro mucho verle á V.
I am very glad to see you.	Me alegro mucho verle á V.
When did you return?	Cuando volvió V?
I thought you were in Boston.	Le creía á V en Boston.
I came home last night.	Llegué aquí ayer á noche.
How did you come?	Como vino?
came by the stage.	Vine en el coche.
came in the mail coach.	Vine con el correo.
You come rather unexpectedly.	V viene cuando ménos se espera.

I thought I would stay all the summer at Philadelphia.	Creía quedarme todo el verano en Filadélfia.
What made you return so soon?	Como volvió tan pronto?
Some business called me here.	Me ha traido aquí un negócio.
How did you like your journey?	Le gustó su viage.
I liked it very well.	Me gustó mucho.
I have had a very pleasant journey.	He tenido un viage muy agradable.
When shall I have the pleasure to see you at my house?	Cuando tendré el gusto de verle en casa?
When will you come and dine with us?	Cuando vendrá á comer con nosotros?
I cannot tell you.	No le puedo decir.
I will go one day or other.	Iré un dia de estos
Come to-day.	Venga hoy.
I cannot.	No puedo.
I have some business to do.	Tengo que* hacer.
I shall wait upon you.	Pasaré á verle.
To call on Mr. Jones sometime to-morrow.	Pasar en casa del señor Jones mañana.
We shall be very happy to see you.	Tendrémos mucho gusto en verle.

Going and Coming. — Para ir, y venir.

Where are you going to?	A donde va?

* Tengo que hacer, I have something to do

I am going home.	Voy á casa.
I was going to your house.	Iba á su casa.
I came from his house.	Vine de su casa.
I was coming from her house.	Venia de su casa.
I am to go to their house.	Voy á su casa
I shall be at home.	Estaré en casa.
You will find him at his house.	Le encontrará en su casa.
I came from your father's.	Vine de casa de su padre.
I shall go to-morrow to my friend's.	Mañana iré á casa de mi amigo.
Where do you come from?	De donde viene V?
I come from Mr. B's.	Vengo de casa del señor B.
I was to go to Paris.	Debia ir á Paris.
I shall perhaps go to France.	Puede ser que vaya á Francia
I am going away, it is time.	Me voy, ya es hora.
I am going to take a walk.	Voy á pasear.
I was going to church.	Iba á la Yglesia.
Will you come with me?	Quiere V acompañarme?
Where do you wish to go to?	A donde quiere V ir?*
Where shall we go to?	A donde irémos?
We will go and take a walk.	Irémos á pasear.

*One verb generally governs another in the infinitive, unless a conjunction intervene.

Let us go to Mr. G's.	Vamos á casa del señor G.
Let us call on Mrs. F.	Pasemos á casa de la señora F.
Let us rather go to the Museum.	Vamos mejor al Museo.
Let us go this way.	Vámos por aquí.
Give me your arm.	Deme el brazo.
Let us cross the street.	Atravesemos la calle.
With all my heart.	De buena gana.
Which way shall we go?	Por donde irémos?
Which way you please.	Por donde V quiera.
I have just left school.	Acabo de dejar la escuela.
Let us go and take a walk.	Vamos á dar un paseo
I have no objection.	No tengo inconveniente.
Let us take your brother on our way.	Tomemos á su hermano, de camino.
Is Mr. B. at home?	Está en casa (el señor B?)
Is Mrs. C. at home?	Está en casa (la señora de C?)
She is just gone out.	Acaba de salir.
He is gone out.	Salió.
He is not at home.	No está en casa.
Can you tell us where he is gone to?	Puede V decirnos á donde fué?
I cannot tell you exactly.	No le puedo decir precisamente.
I think he is gone to see his sister.	Creo que fué á ver á su hermana.
Do you know when he will return?	Sabe V cuando volverá?

No, sir, he said nothing when he went out.	No, señor, no dijo nada cuando salió.
Tell him to come to see him.	Dígale que vénga á verle.
I will come again to-morrow.	Volveré mañana.
When must I call again to find him in?	Cuando volveré para encontrarle en casa?
Call again at four o'clock.	Vuelva V á las cuatro.
Did you return late?	Volvió V tarde?
They have returned from.	Volviéron de . . .
How long will it be before you come back?	Cuanto tardará ántes de volver V?
I shall come back at ten o'clock, at latest.	Volveré á las diez lo mas tarde.
Will you come back again?	Volverá V?
What will you gain by it?	Que le aprovechará á V?
But to return to that.	Pero al asunto.
You will get nothing by it.	No le aprovechará á V nada.
When did you return from the country?	Cuando volvió V del campo?
Come back as fast as you can.	Vuelva lo mas pronto posible.
Come back quickly.	Vuelva pronto.
How much does that come to?	Cuanto cuesta eso?
I shall see you on my return.	Le veré á V cuando vuelva.
When I had returned home.	Cuando habia vuelto á casa.
I must return home.	Necesito volver á casa.

I shall go to New York to-morrow.	Mañana, voy á Nueva York.
I will not fail to go there.	No dejaré de ir allá.
I will go along with you.	Iré con V.
You go too fast.	V anda demasiado pronto
I will go the first opportunity.	Iré la primera ocasion.
So far so good.	Hasta ahora, todo va bien
How far shall we go?	Hasta donde irémos?
Go before.	Vaya V delante.
I will go there from time to time.	Iré allá de cuando en cuando.
Do you believe that he will go there?	Cree V que vaya allí?
I intend going there.	Tengo intencion de ir allá.
I go there twice a week.	Voy allá dos veces la semana.
Will he go with you?	Irá con V?
I believe he is gone home.	Creo que se fué á casa.
All goes well.	Todo va bien.
I am going away.	Me voy.
I went there twice.	Estube allá dos veces.
She is gone into the country.	Se fué al campo.
Do you go to Baltimore.	Va V á Baltimore?
It will soon be time to set out,	Luego será tiempo de marchar.
He has been gone this hour.	Hace una hora que se marchó
Go a little higher up.	Vaya V un poco mas arriba.
Go a little lower down	Vaya V un poco mas abajo.

Come up here quickly.	Suba V aquí pronto.
Come as early as you please.	Venga V á la hora que quiere.
Do not fail to go there.	No falte V en ir allá.
I shall go and see you to-morrow for certain.	Iré á verle á V mañana sin falta.

The Walk. — El Paseo.

Will you go and take a little walk?	Quiere V ir á dar un paseito?
With all my heart.	Con mucho gusto.
I will ask your leave to go and fetch my hat.	Permítame V ir á buscar mi sombrero.
I will be with you in a minute.	Volveré en un instante.
Now I am ready to follow you.	Estoy á sus órdenes.
I am at your command.	Mande V.
We will go when you please.	Irémos cuando V guste.
Which way shall we go?	Por donde irémos.
Let us go across the fields.	Atrevesemos los campos.
I do not like walking on the highway.	No me gusta pasearme en el camino real.
There is always much dust.	Hay siempre mucho polvo.
The rain has laid the dust a little.	La llúvia ha apagado un poco el polvo.
Let us cross the meadow.	Atravesémos el prado.
It is a very pleasant walk.	Es paseo muy agradable.
Under this large oak we	Bajo esta encina grande.

shall be sheltered from the sun.	estarémos al abrigo del sol.
Shall we cross this field?	Atravesaremos este campo?
Is there a thorough-fare across this field?	Se puede pasar por este campo?
Let us take this path.	Tomemos este camino.
It is the nearest way to go home.	Es el mas corca para ir á casa.
It is not late.	No es tarde.
Let us walk a little longer.	Paseémonos un poco mas.
I want to go home in good time.	Quiero volver á casa temprano.
We are not far from the house.	No estamos léjos de la casa.
We shall be there in less than half an hour.	Estarémos allá en ménos de media hora.

Walk in the Garden. — Paseo en el Jardin.

Would you like to take a walk in the garden?	Le gustaria á V pasearse en el jardin?
With great pleasure.	Con mucho gusto.
I am very fond of gardens.	Me gustan mucho los jardines.
The trees have done blowing.	Han acabado los árboles de florecer.
There is a fine show of plums this year.	Hay buena apariencia de ciruelas este año.
What a quantity of apples there will be.	Que de manzanas habrá.
Yes, if one judges by the flowers.	Si, si se puede former una idea por las flores.

WALK IN A GARDEN.

There will be very fine apricots this year.	Habrá hermosos albaricoques este año.
These peaches look well.	Los melocotones estan buenos.
You will have plenty of nectarines.	Tendrá V muchos albérchigos.
Cherries and strawberries are now in their prime.	Es la abundancia de las cerezas y fresas ahora.
They will soon be over.	Pronto pasaran.
These grapes are quite ripe.	Estas uvas estan maduras.
These pears are very fine.	Son muy hermosas las peras.
All the fruits are very early this season.	Todas las frutas son tempranas este año.
The espaliers especially.	Epecialmente las de los espalleres.
How are the trees in your orchard?	Como estan los árboles en su huerta.
They are loaded with fruits.	Estan cargados de fruta.
Let us go now into the flower garden.	Ahora vámos al jardin.
You have not yet seen my flowers.	V no ha visto mis flores.
Come and see my flowers, they are beautiful.	Venga V á ver mis flores, son hermosas.
The garden begins to look pleasant.	El jardin comienza á parecer hermoso.
The flowers come in abundance.	Salen las flores en abundáncia.
The tulips have been in blossom some time.	Los tulipanes hace tiempo que estan en boton.
The narcissus will soon come out.	Los narcisos saldran pronto.

What a fine bed you have of them.	¡Que hermosa plancha tiene V.!
The hyacinths are nearly over.	Los jacintos casi se acabáron.
How do you call this flower?	Como se llama esta flor?
What a beautiful double rose.	¡Que hermosa rosa doble!
Here is a fine cactus.	Aquí hay un cacto hermoso.
Are you fond of carnations?	Le gustan á V. los claveles?
Yes, but I do not like the smell.	Sí, pero no me gusta el olor de ellos.
Here are some pretty fine ones.	Aquí hay algunos muy bonitos.
I like the odour of the violet	Me gusta el olor de la violeta.
That of the rose pleases me pretty well.	Me gusta bastante el olor de la rosa.
You have not seen my ranunculuses.	V. no ha visto mis ranúnculos.
They are astonishingly beautiful.	Son hermosísimos!
You have a very fine collection of flowers.	V. tiene hermosa coleccion de flores.
You keep your garden very neat.	V. tiene todo muy bien arreglado.
Your garden is perfectly well kept.	Su jardin de V. está muy limpio.
Let us see your kitchen garden.	Enséñeme V. su huerta.
How every thing grows.	Como todo crece!

WALK IN A GARDEN.

The rain has done a great deal of good.	La última lluvia ha hecho mucho bien.
There was great need of it.	Nos faltaba mucho.
What a quantity of cabbages!	¡Qué de coles!
What fine cauliflowers!	¡Qué hermosas coliflores
Here is a fine bed of asparagus.	He aquí un hermoso surco de espárragos.
I am very fond of them.	Me gustan mucho.
I like artichokes nearly as well.	Me gústan casi tanto las alcachofas.
These peas are in blossom already.	Los chícharos ya están echando la vaina.
I have some in pods in another place.	Tengo algunos con cáscara en otra parte.
Have you planted any Lima beans?	Ha plantado V. habas de Lima?
You will have some very early.	Las tendrá V. temprano.
What is that?	Qué es eso?
They are carrots and turnips.	Son zanahorias y navos.
What have you there?	Qué tiene V. allí?
I had never seen any before.	Jamas las habia visto.
Are these onions?	Estas son cebollas?
No. they are leeks.	No. son puerros.
They are very much like onions.	Parecen mucho á cebollas.
I see you have all sorts of salad.	Veo que V. tiene todas clases de ensalada.
Here is cabbage lettuce, and cross lettuce.	Aquí hay lechuga de repollo y larga.

This is endive.	Estas son endivas.
I do not see any celery.	No veo apio.
It is in another part of the garden.	Está en otra parte de la huerta.
I think your garden is pretty well stocked.	Su jardin está muy surtido de todo.
You have plenty of every thing.	V. tiene bastante de todo.
It is better to have too much than too little, when one can afford it.	Mejor es tener demasiado que poco, cuando tiene uno los médios.

Evening

La tarde.

It begins to grow late.	Se hace tarde.
It is almost time to go to bed.	Es casi hora de ir a acostarse.
Mr. A... is not come home yet.	El Señor de A... no ha vuelto á casa todavía.
He generally keeps good hours.	Generalmente viene á búena hora.
I hear a knock.	Oigo tocár.
Very likely it is he that knocks.	Parece que es él que toca
Go and see.	Vaya á ver.
Just so, it is he.	Es verdad, él es.
I hope I have not made you wait.	Espero que no le he hecho á V. esperar.
Not in the least.	No, ni un momento.
It is but ten o'clock.	Son solamente las diez.
We never go to bed before half-past ten	Nunca nos acostamos ántes de las diez y media.
How did you find your walk this evening?	¿Como le pareció á V. su paseo de esta tarde?

Very pleasant.	Muy agradable.
It is a charming evening.	Hace una tarde divina.
Are you not tired?	No está V. cansado?
Not much.	Muy poco.
Won't you rest yourself a little?	No quiere V. descansar un poco?
No, I thank you.	No, gracias.
I am going to bed.	Me voy á la cama.
It is not late.	No es tarde.
It is yet early.	Es temprano todavía.
It is time to go to bed.	Es tiempo de acostarse.
I do not like to go to bed late.	No me gusta acostarme tarde.
I like to go to bed in good time.	Me gusta acostarme de buena hora.
I wish you a good night.	Tenga V. buenas noches.
I wish you a good night's rest.	Descanse V. bien.

To write a letter. — Para escribir una carta.

Have the goodness to lend me your penknife.	Hágame V. el favor de prestarme su cortaplumas.
What do you want to do with it?	Para que lo quiere V.?
I want to make a pen to write a letter.	Quiero cortar pluma para escribir una carta.
Why don't you use your own penknife?	Porqué no se sirve V. de su cortaplumas?
It does not cut.	No corta.
It is blunt.	Está embotado.
It wants to be sharpened.	Necesita afilarse.

Have you got letter paper?	Tiene V. papel para escribir?
I have a whole quire.	Tengo un cuadernillo entero.
Do you want any?	Quiere V.?
Lend me a sheet, if you please.	Présteme un pliego si V gusta.
I have a letter to write this evening.	Tengo que escribir una carta esta tarde.
Is it for the mail?	Es para el correo?
Yes, it must go to-day.	Sí, es preciso que vaya hoy.
You have no time to spare, for it is very late already.	No tiene V. tiempo, porque ya es muy tarde.
I shall not be long.	No tardaré mucho.
What day of the month is this?	A cuantos estamos del mes?
What day of the month have we?	En que dia vivimos?
What is the day of the month?	Que dia del mes?
To-day is the first of the month, or the second, or the third, or the fourth, or the fifth, &c.	Hoy tenemos el primero del mes, ó el dos, ó el tres, ó el cuarto, ó el cinco, &a.
Now, I have only the direction to write.	Ahora no tengo mas que poner el sobrescrito.
The letter is not sealed.	La carta no está lacrada.
I have no sealing wax.	No tengo lacre.
Here is a wafer.	Aquí hay oblea.
John, take this letter to the post office.	Juan, lleve esta carta al correo.
Pay the postage of it.	Pague el porte.

The mail was ready to start	Se marchaba el correo
Will my letter go?	Irá mi carta?
Yes, I arrived in good time.	Sí, llegué á tiempo.
Your letter will be to-morrow morning at Baltimore.	Mañana estará su carta en Baltimore.

Needle-Work. — De la costura.

I want a needle.	Me falta una aguja.
What have you to sew?	Que tiene V. que coser?
I am going to mend my gown.	Voy á remendar mi vestido ó bata.
This needle is too large.	Esta aguja es demasiado grande.
Here is another.	Aquí está otra.
This is too small.	Esta es demasiado pequeña.
Give me some thread.	Deme V. hilo.
I have nothing but silk.	No tengo mas que seda.
I have a little cotton left.	Me queda un poco de algodon.
I thought I had some worsted.	Creí que tenia estambre.
What colour do you want it?	Que color quiere V.?
I want it red.	Lo quiero encarnado.
What is it for?	Para que es?
To stitch my collar.	Para atesar el cuello.
Is this the colour you want?	Es esto el color que V. quiere?

This colour is too deep.	Este color es demasiado oscuro.
It will not match.	No liga bien.
It is too light.	Es demasiado claro.
It will match well.	Liga bien.
Have you finished your apron?	Acabó V. su delantal?
Not quite.	Me falta un poco.
I have had something else to do.	He tenido otra cosa que hacer.
I have hemmed my handkerchief.	He dobladillado mi pañuelo.
Then I had my gloves to sew.	Entónces tenia que coser mis guantes.
After that I darned my muslin apron.	Despues he surcido mi delantal de muselina.
Indeed you have been very busy.	De véras V. ha estado bien ocupado.

A Visit. — Una visita.

Somebody knocks.	Toca alguno.
Go and see who it is.	Vaya á ver quién es.
Go and open the door.	Vaya á abrir la puerta.
It is Mr. Butler.	Es el Señor de Butler.
Good morning to you.	Buenos dias tenga V.
I am very glad to see you.	Me alegro mucho verle á V.
I am very happy to see you.	Tengo mucho gusto de verle á V.
I have not seen you for a long time.	Hace mucho tiempo que no le he visto.
You are quite a stranger.	Es V. estrangero.

Pray be seated.	Hágame V el favor de sentarse.
Give a chair to this gentleman.	Dé una silla al Señor.
Will you stay and take some dinner with us?	Quiere V quedarse á comer con nosotros?
I cannot stay.	No puedo quedarme.
I only came down to know how you did.	Vine solamente á saber como lo pasaba V.
I must go.	Es preciso que me vaya.
You are in a great hurry.	Tiene V. mucha prisa.
Why are you in such a hurry?	Porqué tiene V. tanta prisa?
I have a great many things to do.	Tengo muchas cosas que hacer.
Sure you can stay a little longer.	Seguro, puede V. quedarse un poco mas.
I have many places to call at.	Tengo que pasar á muchos puntos.
I will stay longer another time.	Me quedaré mas otra vez.
I thank you for your visit.	Gracias de su visita.

Drawing. — El dibujo.

Drawing is my favourite occupation.	El dibujo es mi ocupacion favorita.
I am passionately fond of it.	Soy muy apasionado á él.
I could spend whole days at it without being tired.	Pasaria dias enteras dibujando, sin cansarme.
It is certainly a very pleasant accomplishment.	Es ciertamente un ornamento agradable.
It is likewise very useful.	Tambien es muy útil.

Particularly in some professions.	Sobretodo en algunas artes.
How long have you been learning?	Cuanto hace que V. aprende?
Your sister draws very well.	Su hermana de V. dibuja bien.
In what style do you best succeed?	En qué estilo dibuja V. mejor?
What is your favourite style?	Cuál es su estilo favorito?
Landscape is what I most admire.	El paysaje es lo que mas admiro.
As for me, I prefer figures; in fact, I have seen figures of yours in crayon, which pleased me very much.	Yo prefiero el natural; en efecto, he visto obras suyas de creyon, que me gustáron muchisimo.
Have you ever attempted flowers?	Ha ensayado V. alguna vez las flores?
I will show you some of my attempts in that style.	Le enseñaré algunos ensayos mios en ese estilo.
I do not know sufficiently how to colour them.	No conozco bastante bien la aplicacion del colorido.
Flowers, simply drawn in crayon, produce no considerable effect.	Las flores dibujadas simplemente á creyon, producen poco efecto.
This is beautiful.	Eso es hermoso.
I hope you will not neglect so extraordinary a talent.	Espero que V. se aprovechará de tan estraordinario talento.
You will excel.	V. será sobresaliente

Will you show me your portfolio?	Enséñeme V. su cartera
Here are very beautiful pieces.	Aquí hay muy hermosas piezas.
Did you do this drawing without the assistance of your master?	Hizo V. este dibujo sin ayuda del maestro?
He touched it up a little.	El lo ha perfeccionado un poco.
Have you the fine collection of Raphael's drawings?	Tiene V. la hermosa coleccion de las pinturas de Rafael?
No, but I have some of Rubens. Titian, Poussin, Guido, Romano, and several other great masters.	No, pero tengo algunas de Reubens, Ticiano, Poussin, Guido, Romano y otros varios maestros.
This is a precious collection.	Es una coleccion preciosa.

At an Exhibition of Paintings.
En una exhibicion de pinturas.

Is there any collection of paintings in this town?	Hay alguna coleccion de pinturas en esta villa?
Is there an annual public exhibition of paintings in this place?	Hay alguna exhibicion anual de pinturas en este pueblo?
Yes Sir; I hope you will be pleased with it.	Sí, Señor; espero que la gustará á V.
When will the exhibition take place?	Cuando será la exhibicion?
It is open now.	Está abierta ahora.

Let us go there.	Vamos allá.
I have a passion for pictures.	Soy apasionado por la pintura.
That painting is a copy from Raphael.	Esa pintura es una copia de Rafael.
This is from Poussin.	Esta es de Poussin.
This is a copy from Titian.	Esta es una copia del Ticiano.
Titian excelled in colouring.	Ticiano sobresalió en el colorido.
And in drawing likewise.	Y tambien en el dibujo.
There is a fine distribution in that picture.	Hay una escelente distribucion de colores en esa pintura.
Its composition is fine.	El todo es escelente.
This is an historical picture.	Es un cuadro histórico
This is a well-executed painting.	Es un cuadro bien ejecutado.
The passions are well marked.	Las pasiones estan bien representadas.
How do you like the foreground?	Que le parece á V. de ese claro?
That picture requires to be seen in its proper light.	Esa pintura necesita buscarle su punto de vista.
It is not in its proper light.	Este no es su punto de vista.
It is not in its proper situation.	No está bien colocada.
That picture is deficient in colouring.	Le falta color á esa pintura.
That painter draws better than he colours.	Ese pintor dibuja mejor que colorea.

AT AN EXHIBITION OF PAINTINGS.

These colours are too lively.	Esos colores son demasiado alegres.
They should have been subdued.	Debian ser un poco mas sombreados.
There is a fine tone of colour in that picture.	Hay gusto en los colores de ese cuadro.
This valuable picture is in fine preservation.	Esta pintura preciosa está bien conservada.
How well the lights and shades are distributed!	¡Qué bien distribuidas estan las luces y las sombras.
That painter understands well the disposition of the lights.	Ese pintor conoce perfectamente la distribucion de las sombras.
It is in the style of Rembrandt.	Es en el estilo de Rembrandt.
That great master formed a style adapted to great effects	Ese gran maestro tiene un estilo que causa gran efecto.
A landscape forms the back ground to the figures of that picture.	Un paysage forma la sombra detras de las figuras.
This is in water colours.	Tiene colores de agua.
That drawing is from nature.	Ese dibujo está tomado del natural.
That artist understands very well the effect of light and shade.	Este artista entiende perfectamente el efecto de la luz y la sombra
Those figures are in the middle-tint.	Esas figuras estan á media tinta.
That painter succeeds better in portrait than in historical painting.	Ese pintor hace mejores retratos que cuadros nistóricos

Have you seen that pencil-sketch?	Ha visto V. aquel bosquejo de lápiz?
No. I was considering this drawing in Indian ink.	No, estaba mirando este dibujo con tinta de China.
I like oil painting better.	Me gustan mas las pinturas al olio.
There are two very beautiful sea pieces near the window.	Hay dos hermosas vistas marítimas cerca de la ventana.
The reflections in the water are admirable.	Los reflejos en el agua son admirables.
See those clouds, how skilfully the lights are managed.	Mire V. esas nubes. ¡que diestramente alumbradas estan!
I am delighted with all I have seen.	Me ha divertido todo lo que he visto.
I think we have seen everything.	Creo que hemos visto todo.
Let us go away.	Vámonos.
We will come again tomorrow.	Volverémos mañana

Expressions of Surprise. — Espresiones de sorpresa.

What!	Que!
Truly!	De véras!
Is it possible!	Es posible!
Could it be possible!	Será posible.
It is really possible!	Sí, es posible!
How can that be!	Como puede ser eso!
How is that possible!	Como es posible!
That is impossible!	Eso es imposible!
It is not possible!	No es posible!

That cannot be!	Eso no puede ser!
I cannot think how ...!	No puedo imaginarme como ...!
I am surprised at it!	Me sorprende!
I am quite astonished at it!	Estoy enteramente admirado!
That surprises me!	Eso me sorprende!
You surprise me!	V. me sorprende!
You astonish me!	V. me admira!
This is what surprises me!	Eso es lo que me sorprende á mí!
That quite astonishes me!	Eso me admira mucho!
I wonder at it!	Estraño mucho eso!
This is quite astonishing!	Eso es muy estraño!
It is inconceivable!	Es increible!
It is a thing not to be conceived!	Es una cosa que no se puede concebir!
That is unheard of!	Nunca se ha oido!
It is a thing unheard of!	Es cosa que nunca se ha oido!
That is very strange!	Eso es muy estraño!
That is a strange sort of a business, indeed!	De véras, eso es negocio muy estraño!
That is something strange!	Es cosa estraña!

Expressions of Probability.

Espresiones de Probabilidad.

That is probable.	Eso es probable.
That is likely.	Se parece.
That is likely.	Eso puede ser.
It is likely enough.	Bien puede ser.
That is not unlikely.	Eso no es improbable.
It is not at all unlikely.	Eso bien puede ser.

That is very probable.	Eso es muy probable.
That is more than probable.	Eso es mas que probable.
There is nothing impossible in it.	No hay nada de imposible en eso.
That is not impossible.	Eso no es imposible.
I see nothing impossible in it.	No veo nada de imposible en eso.
That is not impossible.	Eso no es imposible.
That may be.	Eso puede ser.
That might be so.	Eso podia ser.
I do not wonder at it.	No estraño eso.
I am not surprised at it.	No me sorprende eso.
That does not astonish me	No me admira eso.
That does not surprise me.	Eso no me sorprende
It is not astonishing.	No es admirable.
It is not surprising.	No es sorprendente.
There is nothing surprising in it.	No hay nada de sorprendente en eso,
You do not astonish me,	V. no me admira.
You do not surprise me,	V. no me sorprende.
I do not wonder at it.	No estraño eso,
I should not wonder at it,	No me estrañaria.
That would not surprise me	Eso no me sorprenderia.
Of course it is natural,	Por supuesto, es muy natural.
No wonder,	No hay nada de estraño.
It is a matter of course,	Es cosa regular.
That is understood.	Eso se entiende.

Expressions of Joy.

Espresiones de Alegria.

I am much pleased.	Me da mucho gusto.
I am very glad.	Me alegro mucho.

I am very happy.	Estoy muy contento.
I am delighted.	Estoy deleitado.
We were in raptures.	Eso nos arrebató.
I am extremely happy to hear it.	Me alegro mucho oirlo.
They are very glad of it.	Se alégran mucho de eso.
It gives me great joy,	Me da muchísimo gusto.
It makes me very happy to hear it.	Me complace el oirlo.
It gives her a great deal of joy.	Se le causa mucha alegría.
It gives the greatest pleasure.	Causa el mayor placer.
We congratulate you upon it.	Felicitamos á V. por esto
I wish you joy with all my heart.	Deseo su bienestar de todo mi corazon.
I sincerely wish you joy.	Deseo sinceramente su alegría.
I congratulate you upon it.	Le doy la enhorabuena.

Expressions of Sorrow.

Expresiones de Sentimiento.

I am sorry for it.	Lo siento.
I am very sorry for it.	Lo siento mucho.
I am quite vexed at it.	Me pesa mucho. (*)
I am extremely sorry for it	Lo siento muchísimo
I am quite inconsolable.	Estoy inconsolable.
It makes me quite unhappy.	Causa mi infelicidad.
It vexes me beyond ex-	Me mortifica fuera de to-

(*) *Pesar.* to weigh

pression. | da ponderacion

What a pity!	Que lástima.
It is a very great pity.	Es una lástima!
It is a sad thing.	Es una cosa bien triste
It is a melancholy case.	Es un caso melancólico
That is a quite vexing.	Eso es muy molesto.
That is very disagreeble.	Es muy desagradable.
It is very provoking.	Es muy provocativo.
It is a cruel case.	Es caso muy cruel.
That is very hard.	Eso es muy duro.
This is shocking.	Eso hace temblar.
That is very unlucky.	Eso es un infortunio.
It is a great misfortune.	Es una grande desgracia.
It is dreadful.	Es horroroso.
It makes one's hair stand on end.	Hace herizar los cabellos.

Expressions of Blame. | Expresiones de Censura.

Fie! for shame!	Quita!
Are you not ashamed?	No tienes vergüenza?
Are you not ashamed of yourself?	No se avergüenza V. de sí mismo?
You ought to be ashamed.	V. debia avergonzarse.
I am ashamed of you.	Me avergüenzo de V.
What a shame!	¡Que vergüenza!
It is shameful.	Es vergonzoso.
It is a shameful thing.	Es cosa vergonzosa.
It is very bad.	Es muy malo.
How naughty that is	¡Que malo es eso!
That is very wicked.	Eso es muy perverso.
It is abominable.	Es abominable.
How can you be so wicked?	Como puede V. ser tan malvado?

How could you do so?	Como ha podido V. hacerlo?
How came you to do so?	Como vino V. á hacer eso?
You are very bad.	Es V. muy malo.
Why did you do that?	Porqué ha hecho V. eso?
One must be very bad.	Ha de ser uno muy malo
One must be very naughty.	Se ha de ser muy perverso.

Expressions of Anger. — Expresiones de cólera.

I am very angry.	Estoy* muy enfadado.
I am not in a good humour.	No estoy de buen humor.
He is very cross.	Está de muy mal humor.
I am affronted with him.	Estoy enfadado con él.
I am quite stung.	Estoy enteramente ofendido.
I am quite exasperated.	Estoy ecsasperado.
I am beside myself.	Estoy fuera de mí.
You see me in a terrible passion.	Estoy furioso.
It makes me quite mad.	Me vuelve loco.
I cannot contain myself for anger.	No puedo contenerme de cólera.
That is very bad of you.	Hace V. muy mal.
You are very much to be blamed.	Es V. muy culpable.
You are quite wrong.	V. está equivocado.
How did you dare to do so?	Cómo se atrevió V. á hacerlo?

---

* Observe the use of the verb *estar*, implying a temporary state.

EXPRESSIONS OF ANGER

I am not satisfied with you.	No estoy satisfecho de V
I am quite dissatisfied with you.	Estoy descontento de V.
I shall be very angry.	Estaré muy enfadado.
Be quiet.	Estate quieto.
Have done, I say.	Acabaras!
Can you not be quiet?	No puedes estarte quieto?
Be easy.	Tranquilícese* V.
Be at rest.	Repósese.
I tell you beforehand that	Le prevengo á V que ...
I warn you about it.	Le advierto á V
Pay attention to what I say.	Atienda V. á lo que le digo.
Mind what I told you.	Tenga V. presente lo que le he dicho.
I will not have that.	No lo quiero.
I will not suffer that	No lo sufriré.
I will have it so.	Yo lo quiero así.
I insist upon it.	Lo quiero absolutamente
Mind for another time.	Cuidado para otra ocasion
Do not do so any more.	No lo vuelva V. á hacer
Don't be saucy.	No seas impertinente
Silence! hold your tongue.	Silencio! cállese† V.
Will you hold your tongue?	Se callará V.?
No reasonings.	No mas razones.
Do not reply.	No replique V.
Get out of my sight.	Retírese V. de mi vista ó quítate de mi presencia.

---

* Pronoun after the verb in the Imperative affirmative and Infinitive.
† *Callarse*, to be silent.

I will see you no more.	No quiero verle mas.
I do not like disobedient children.	No me gustan los niños desobedientes.
Your conduct does not admit of any apology.	Tu conducta no admite escusa.
This is the tenth time you have disobeyed me.	Esta es la décima vez que me has desobedecido.

Expressions of Antipathy and Aversion. / Expresiones de antipatia y aversion.

I do not like that man.	No me gusta aquel hombre.
I detest that man.	Detesto á ese hombre.
I cannot bear that man	No puedo sufrir á ese hombre.
His manners are repelling.	Sus modales son chocantes.
He has not a pleasing countenance.	No tiene una cara agradable.
His look is not prepossessing.	Su figura no le recomienda.
There is something displeasing in his address.	En su modo de presentarse, se nota un no sé qué de repugnante.
I cannot restrain the aversion I feel for him.	No puedo ménos de demostrar la aversion que siento hácia él.
He has no notion of propriety.	No tiene ni una nocion de delicadeza
He has not the least notion of propriety.	No tiene la menor idea de finura.
He has no regard for anybody.	No se le da por nadie.

That makes him to be hated.	Esto le hace odioso.
He is hated by everybody for it.	Todo el mundo le aborrece por eso.
I avoid him as much as I can.	Le huyo cuanto puedo.
He tires me to death.	Su presencia me mata.
His language is offensive.	Tiene una lengua viperina.
He talks most extravagantly.	Su lenguage es el mas extravagante.
He likes to dictate everywhere.	Le gusta mandar en todas partes.
What an insupportable being!	¡Qué hombre tan insoportable!
What a tiresome character!	¡Qué carácter tan nauseabundo!
Shall we never be able to get rid of him?	Nunca podrémos deshacernos de él?
I wish he would go.	Me alegraria que se fuera
At last he is gone.	Por fin se fué.

Expressions of Sympathy and Friendship.

Expresiones de simpatía y amistad.

He is my friend.	Es amigo mio.
He is my best friend.	Es mi mejor amigo.
He is my intimate friend.	Es mi amigo íntimo.
We are intimate friends.	Somos íntimos amigos.
I am sincerely attached to him.	Le quiero sinceramente.
Our friendship is reciprocal.	Nuestra amistad es recíproca.
Our tempers are alike.	Nuestros génios son iguales.

We are closely united.	Somos estrechamente unidos.
We agree perfectly well.	Estamos perfectamente de acuerdo.
He has given me many proofs of his friendship.	Me ha dado muchas pruebas de su amistad.
I hope we shall never part.	Espero que jamas nos separarémos.
I felt an attachment for him the first time I met him.	He sympatizado con él desde la primera vez que le he visto.
We love each other like brothers.	Nos querémos como hermanos.
There is no secret between us.	No hay secreto entre nosotros dos.
We have no secret for each other.	No tenemos secreto el uno para el otro.
I would do anything for him.	Haria cuanto pudiese para servirle.

With the Tailor. — Con el Sastre.

Somebody wants to speak to you.	Preguntan por V.
Who is it?	Quien es?
Who wants to speak to me?	Quien me quiere hablar?
It is the tailor.	Es el sastre.
Bid him come up.	Dígale que suba.*
I have sent for you to measure me for a coat.	Le he mandado á V. buscar, para tomarme la medida de una levita.

---

* *Suba*, subjunctive depending on *Diga*

WITH THE TAILOR.

I want a coat.	Quiero una levita.
I require a coat.	Me hace falta una levita.
I want a suit of clothes.	Quiero un vestido entero.
Take my measure.	Tómeme V. la medida.
Will you take my measure?	Me quiere V. tomar la medida.
Take my measure for a coat.	Tómeme la medida de una casaca.
How will you have it made?	Como la quiere V.?
As they are worn now.	Como se usan ahora.
In the newest fashion.	De la última moda.
I shall want a waistcoat and a pair of trowsers.	Necesito chaleco* y pantalones.
But I should like to see a few patterns.	Pero quisiera ver algunas muestras.
Show me some patterns.	Déjeme ver algunas muestras.
Have you brought some with you?	Ha traido V. algunas?
I have a great variety.	Tengo un gran surtido.
Let me see them.	Déjeme verlas.
You may choose which you like best.	Puede V. escojer las que le gusten.
I like this fine blue well enough.	Me gusta este azul fino.
It is a colour which is much in fashion.	Es color muy de moda.
Green will become you very well.	El verde le viene† á V muy bien.
What do you think of this green?	Que le parece de este verde?

---

* Article indefinite often omitted in Spanish
† Venir, to come.

WITH THE TAILOR

I should prefer a bottle-green.	Prefiero un verde oscuro.
That colour will soon fade.	Ese color pierde pronto.
I want also two waistcoats.	Quiero tambien dos chalecos.
Will you have silk or cassimere?	Los quiere V. de seda ó de casimir?
You will make one of cassimere, and the other of silk.	Uno de casimir, y el otro de seda
What cassimere will you have, double or single milled?	Que casimir quiere V., doble ó sencillo?
I prefer the single milled, it fits better.	Prefiero el sencillo, sienta* mejor.
What sort of buttons will you have to your coat?	Que clase de botones quiere V. en la levita?
Will you have covered buttons?	Quiere V. botones cubiertos?
Shall I put silk buttons to it?	Quiere V. que ponga botones de seda?
No; I prefer gilt buttons, if they are fashionable.	No; quiero botones dorados, si son de moda.
Do you wear your trowsers very high?	Usa V. pantalones muy subidos?
Neither too high nor too low.	Ni muy subidos ni muy bajos.
Let them come up about so high.	Que lleguen hasta aquí.
I like them very low.	Me gustan muy bajos.
It is the fashion to wear them very low.	Se úsan muy bajos.

* Sentar, to sit. Sentarse, to sit down.

I do not like them too low.	No me gustan demasiado bajos.
Remember, I must have everything the day after to-morrow.	Cuidado, que necesito todo para pasado mañana.
Sir, I shall be punctual.	Señor, seré exacto.
Sir, I bring your coat.	Señor le traigo á V. su levita.
I am glad you have kept your word.	Me alegro que V. haya guardado su palabra.
I want it this morning.	La necesito esta mañana.
I began to be impatient.	Comenzaba á impacientarme.
I have just finished it.	La he acabado ahora mismo.
I hope it will please you.	Espero que le gustará á V.
Let me try it on.	Déjeme ponerla.
Let me see whether it fits me.	A ver si me viene bien.
It fits me very well.	Me viene muy bien.
It makes you a very good shape.	Le sienta á V. muy bien
Are not the sleeves too long and too wide?	No son demasiado largas y anchas las mangas?
They are worn so now	Son de moda ahora.
It is too tight.	Me aprieta demasiado.
It is too tight.	Está demasiado apretado.
It will become wide enough.	Se pondra bastante ancha.
It cuts me under the arms.	Me mortifica debajo de los brazos.
I think it is too long.	Me parece demasiado largo.

The waistcoat is not well made.	No está bien hecho el chaleco.
It is too short.	Es demasiado corto.
The waistcoat and the coat must be altered.	El chaleco y la casaca, es necesario arreglarlos mejor.
I do not see any alteration to make.	No veo nada que componerles.
You cannot complain of this coat.	No puede V. quejarse de esta levita.
Look in the glass.	Mírese V. en el espejo.
It fits you as well as can be.	Es imposible que le esté mejor.
I have a mind to have another coat.	Tengo gana de mandar hacer otra levita.
Call here to-morrow morning; we will go together to buy some cloth.	Pase V. aquí mañana; irémos juntos para comprar paño.
At what time am I to call, sir.	A qué hora quiere V. que venga, Señor?
At about ten.	A eso de las diez.
At about eleven.	Cerca de las once.
Between twelve and one.	Entre las doce y la una.

At a Woollen-draper's. — En casa del Mercader de Paño.

I want to buy some cloth.	Quiero comprar paño.
What sort of cloth do you want?	Que clase de paño quiere V.?
Show me the best you have	Enséñeme lo mejor que tenga.

What colour do you prefer?	Que color prefiere V.?
I like this colour pretty well.	Este color me gusta bastante.
Is it fashionable?	Es de moda?
Blue and black are always fashionable.	Azul y negro estan siempre de moda.
Show me some others.	Enséñeme otros.
Here are patterns of all the superfine cloth I have in my shop.	Aquí tiene V. muestras de todos los paños finos que tengo en la tienda
This colour will soon fade.	Este color pierde* pronto.
Excuse me, Sir; it will wear very well.	Perdone V., Señor; durará mucho.
This cloth is very thin.	Este paño es muy delgado
Here is another piece.	Aquí hay otra pieza
It feels very soft	Es muy suave.
It is substantial.	Es fuerte.
This will do.	Este me conviene.
How much do you ask for it?	Cuanto pide V. por él?
How much do you sell it at a yard?	A como vende V. la vara
Five dollars.	A cinco pesos.
Is that the lowest price?	Eso es lo mas barato?
Cut me three yards	Córteme tres varas.
Here is your money.	Aquí tiene V. su dinero.

At a Linen-draper's.	En casa del Mercader de Paño.
Will you show me some	Quiere V. enseñarme

---

* *Perder*, to lose.

AT A LINEN-DRAPER'S.

Irish linen of the best quality?	tela Irlandesa de la mejor calidad.
Here are several pieces.	Aquí tiene V. várias piezas.
Do you prefer fine Holland?	Le gusta á V. la tela de Holanda?
I will show you some.	Le enseñaré á V. algunas.
It will cost you more.	Le costará á V. mas.
Yes, but it is wider.	Sí, pero es mas ancho.
Here is a piece at one dollar, one at one and a half, and the other at two dollars.	Aquí tiene V. una pieza á peso, otra á peso y medio, y la otra á dos pesos.
This is rather thin.	Este es un poco delgado.
Give me leave to unfold this piece.	Permítame desplegar esta pieza.
I think you will allow it to be fine.	Creo que V. dirá que es fina.
This is a fine white.	Esta es de un blanco fino
What is the price of it?	Cual es el precio?
That cloth seems to me very dear.	Este paño me parece demasiado caro.
It will wear well.	Durará mucho.
Give me these two pieces.	Tomaré estas dos piezas.
Do you want any French cambric?	Quiere V. comprar batista?
I have some fine French cambric, which is not dear.	Tengo batista fina, que no es cara.
How many yards do you want?	Cuantas varas quiere V.?
Permit me to show you some fine tablecloths and napkins.	Permítame V. enseñarle manteles finos y servilletas

They are of a new pattern.	Son de modelos nuevos
They are indeed very handsome.	De véras son muy lindas
But I do not want any.	Pero no necesito.
Have you any good French cambric pocket handkerchiefs?	Tiene V. buenos pañuelos de batista?
Yes, Sir, and I am sure they will please you.	Sí Señor, y estoy seguro que le gustarán á V.
I will take four dozen.	Tomaré cuatro docenas.
Have them marked with my initials, and send me the whole to-morrow.	Mándelos* V. marcar con mis iniciales, y envíamelos todos mañana.

At a Perfumer's. — En casa del Perfumista.

Mrs. B. has directed me to your shop.	La Señora de B. me ha dirijido á su tienda.
Is your shop well stocked with perfumery?	Tiene V. buen surtido de perfumes?
What articles do you keep?	Que artículos vende V.?
I have everything you can desire.	Tengo todo lo que V. pueda desear.
My stock is as complete as it can be.	Tengo un surtido de todo.
I want a few pounds of powder.	Necesito algunas libras de polvos.
Will you have it scented?	Los quiere V. perfumados?

---

* Mandar hacer una cosa, to have a thing made, or to order a thing to be made

Yes, show me some jessamine.	Sí, enséñeme los de jazmin.
The scent is not too strong.	El olor no es demasiado fuerte.
It will suit me.	Me conviene.
I have also violet, rose, and orange-flower.	Tengo tambien de violeta, de rosa, y de flor de naranja.
I want also some lavender and Cologne water.	Quiero tambien de espliego, y de agua de Colónia.
Have you any essential oils?	Tiene V. eséncias de aceyte?
Yes, madam, several sorts.	Sí Señora, muchas clases.
This is of a superior quality.	Este es de una calidad muy superior
How much do you sell this oil of roses for?	A como vende V. este aceite de rosa?
That is very dear.	Es muy caro.
It is too dear.	Es demasiado caro.
It is extravagantly dear.	Es carísimo.
I can buy some elsewhere for less.	Puedo comprar mas barato en otra parte.
It is the usual price.	Es el precio regular.
It is a set price.	Es precio fijo.
I must have also a bottle of orange-flower.	Necesito tambien una botella de flor de naranja.
I now have all I want.	Ahora tengo todo lo que me faltaba.
Give me my account.	Déme V. mi cuenta.
It amounts to ...	Sube á ..
Here is your money, and my address.	Aquí está el dinero, y el número de mi casa.
Send me all these articles.	Envíemelo V. todo.

At a Bookseller's. | En casa del librero.

Have you any new books?	Tiene V. obras nuevas?
I should like to see the books you have just received.	Quisiera ver los libros que V. acaba* de recibir
With great pleasure, Sir, they were unpacked just now.	Señor, con mucho gusto, ahora mismo los acaba de sacar de las cajas.
They are books of history, mathematics, philosophy, divinity, physic, and law.	Son libros de historia, matemáticas, filosofía, teología, medecina, y leyes.
Are all these new books?	Son todas obras nuevas?
No, Sir; some are new, some are old publications.	No Señor; algunas son publicaciones nuevas, otras viejas.
I hope you will find some to suit your taste.	Espero que V. encontrará algunas de su gusto
Here is a note of the books I wish to have.	Aquí tiene V. la lista de los libros que quiero comprar.
Have you now the Buffon that I asked you for?	Tiene V. ahora el Buffon que le pedí?
I have only the 18mo. edition.	Tengo solamente la edicion décimo-octava
It is embellished with coloured plates.	Está adornada de láminas pintadas.
Show me some volumes of Rollin.	A ver algunos tomos de Rollin.
They will bring you some immediately.	Se los traeran á V. al instante.

---

* Acabo de comer, I finish from to dine, or I have just dined.

AT A BOOKSELTER'S.

Here are some.	Aquí hay algunos.
This size pleases me well enough.	Este tamaño me gusta bastante.
I would like to have it bound.	Me gustarian encuadernados.
I will have them bound in calf, and lettered.	Los quiero encuadernados en becerrillo, y rotulados.
I wish to have the edges marbled.	Quisiera los puntos color de mármol.
Show me some of your handsomest bound in Russia leather.	Enséñeme de sus mas hermosos, encuadernados á la Rusa.
Here are the best we have at present.	Aquí ve V. los mejores que tenemos ahora.
This pattern pleases me exceedingly	Esta clase me gusta muchísimo.
I wish this Virgil to be bound in morocco.	Quiero que este Virgílio sea encuadernado en marroquí.
Is the price the same for all colours?	Todos los colores son del mismo precio?
Exactly the same.	Precisamente.
Then I will have it bound in green.	Entónces lo quiero verde
What do they cost?	Cuanto cuestan?
Have you Fenelon's works complete?	Tiene V. las obras de Fenelon completas?
We have the finest edition.	Tenemos la mas bella edicion.
I wish to have the travels of young Anacharsis.	Quiero los viages del jóven Anachársis.
I have one in octavo, but it is only in boards.	Tengo uno en octavo, pero á la rústica.

Have you the Atlas belonging to it?	Tiene V. el Átlas que le pertenece?
We have the quarto Atlas of Tardieu.	Tenemos el Átlas de Tardieu, en cuarto.
I will take it; but you will have it bound in Russia leather.	Lo tomaré; pero ha de ser encuadernado con tafilete de Rúsia.
Here is a fine edition of Bossuet.	Aquí tiene V. una hermosa edicion de Bossuet.
I see in your catalogue a great many splendid editions at a very high price.	Veo en su catálogo muchas ediciones magníficas á precio muy elevado.
Have you Moliere in a small size?	Tiene V. Moliere de un tamaño diminuto.
I have the stereotype edition, on four different kinds of paper.	Tengo la edicion estereotypa, en cuatro clases de papel.
This edition on large vellum paper is beautifully bound.	Esta edicion de papel grande de vitela, está muy bien encuadernada.
I think I had better take the large vellum paper.	Me parece que haria mejor en tomar la de papel grande de vitela.
Here is a very pretty copy.	Aquí hay una copia muy bonita.
It is bound in green morocco, with gilt edges.	Está encuadernada en marroquí verde, con el borde dorado.
I have romances and novels, theatrical productions, reviews, &c.	Tengo romances y novelas, producciones teatrales, revistas, &a.
Oh! I will not have any.	Oh! no quiero de esos.

Sir, do you want anything else?	Señor, necesita V. otra cosa?
I want a copy of Racine; but I do not see any.	Quiero una copia de Racine; pero no veo ninguna.
I have several, but they are in sheets.	Tengo muchas, pero no estan encuadernadas.
What sort of binding do you choose?	Como las quiere V. encuadernadas?
Will you have them in calf or in sheep?	Las* quiere V. en becerrillo ó en pasta?
Half-binding will do; but they must be lettered like that Moliere.	Bastará media pasta; pero han de ser rotuladas como ese Moliere.
Sir, I will take care they shall be done as you direct.	Señor, tendré cuidado de que todo se haga como V. lo ordena.
Have you a plan of Paris?	Tiene V. el plan de Paris?
I wish to have the best and the most correct that is published.	Quiero el mejor y mas correcto que se ha publicado.
Send me everything in the course of the day.	Mándeme todo hoy en todo el dia.
I intend to leave Paris to-morrow morning	Me marcho de Paris mañana por la mañana.

At a Jeweller's.

En casa del Joyero.

Will you show me your rings?	Quiere V. enseñarme sus sortijas?
Are these set with fine stones?	Estas estan montadas con finas piedras?

---

* *Las* referring to *copias*, feminine plural.

AT A JEWELLER'S

What is the price of this ring?	Cuanto vale esta sortija?
It is much too dear	Es carísima.
That diamond has a beautiful lustre.	Ese diamante tiene un lustre muy brillante.
That ring pleases me much.	Esa sortija me gusta mucho.
I think it is too large for me.	Creo que es demasiado grande.
Show me some others.	Déjeme ver otras.
This fits me well.	Esta me viene bien.
Is it firmly mounted?	Está montada fuerte?
What do you ask for it?	Cuanto pide V. por ella?
I prefer the first.	Prefiero la otra.
Can you lessen it?	Puede V. acortarla?
Very easily, and without injuring the mounting.	Muy facilmente, y sin dañar á la montura.
I want a gold chain.	Quisiera una cadena de oro.
Mine is no longer in fashion.	Ya no es de moda, la mia
I can take it in exchange.	Yo la tomaré en cambio.
What will you allow me for mine?	En cuanto me toma* V la mia?
I will weigh it.	La pesaré.
If I exchange my chain, I must exchange my seal too.	Si cambio la cadena, me es preciso tambien cambiar el sello.
Here are several seals of the newest fashion.	Aquí hay varios sellos, de la última moda.
I will take these two.	Tomaré estos dos.

---

* In Spanish, the Present is often used instead of the Future. I will buy those segars of you at twenty-two dollars a thousand: Le compro a V (I buy) esos tabacos á veinte y dos pesos el millar

AT A JEWELLER'S.

I should wish to have my initials engraved upon this seal.	Quiero que se graben mis iniciales en este sello.
Will you undertake to get it engraved?	Los mandará V. grabar?
I will give it to the most skilful engraver we have.	Lo daré al grabador el mas esperimentado que tenemos.
Show me some ear-rings.	Déjeme ver algunos pendientes.
Here are some of exquisite workmanship.	Aquí tiene V. algunos de trabajo esquisito.
Here is a superb necklace.	Aquí hay collar magnífico.
It is not for sale.	No está de venta.
I have just sold it to a lady.	Acabo de venderlo á una Señora.
These bracelets are for the same lady.	Estos brazales son para la misma Señora.
What is the price of this pin?	Cuanto vale* este alfiler?
Are these pins of a new fashion?	Estan de moda estos alfileres?
This topaz surrounded with pearls pleases me much more.	Este topacio cercado de perlas, me gusta mucho mas.
It is very beautiful.	Es hermosísimo.
I think it is stronger.	Me parece mas fuerte.
I have something else to show you.	Tengo otra cosa que enseñarle á V.
No, I thank you, I will come another day.	No, gracias, volveré otro dia.

---

* Valer, to be worth.

At a Watchmaker's. | En casa del Relojero.

I am not pleased with the watch you sold me.	No me gusta el relox que V. me vendió.
Yet I took it on your word.	Sinembargo la tomé bajo su palabra.
It does not go right.	No anda bien.
It goes too fast.	Adelanta.
It goes too slow.	Atrasa.
I cannot regulate it.	No puedo arreglarlo.
It is a new watch.	Este es un relox nuevo.
It will require some time to regulate it.	Se necesita algun tiempo para arreglarlo.
I am willing to believe it.	Ya lo creo.
If you are not satisfied I will change it.	Si V. no está satisfecho, lo cambiaré.
Here is a very good watch	Aquí hay un relox muy bueno.
It shows, besides, the days of the month.	Ademas, enseña los dias del mes.
I do not like such complicated watches.	No me gustan relojes tan complicados.
They are often out of order.	Se descomponen muy a menudo.
I want a good repeater.	Quisiera un buen relox de repeticion.
I have an excellent one.	Tengo uno, excelente.
Will you warrant it?	Lo garantiza V.?
Will you let me have it upon trial?	Me lo permite V. á prueba?
I will only take it upon those terms.	Lo tomo solamente bajo estos términos.
I agree to it with pleasure	Convengo, con gusto.

AT A WATCHMAKER'S.

I give it to you upon trial.	Se lo daré á V. á prueba.
Since I have had it. it has not varied one minute.	Despues que lo tengo, no ha variado un minuto.
You will be pleased with it.	V. estará contento con él.
I can warrant it.	Yo lo garantizo.
How much do you want to boot?	Cuanto quiere V. sobre él?
I have a watch at home which wants cleaning.	Tengo un relox en casa, que necesita limpiarse.
It is an old watch	Es un relox viejo.
It has not gone this fortnight.	Se ha parado, hace quince dias.
I let it fall.	Lo dejé caer.
I think the mainspring is broken.	Creo que se rompió el muelle real.
I will send it to you to-day.	Se lo mandaré á V. hoy.
I must keep it a few days.	Es preciso tenerlo algunos dias.
When will you return it?	Cuando me lo devolverá V.?
I cannot promise it you before a fortnight.	No puedo prometerlo ántes de quince dias.
It is a long time.	Es mucho tiempo.
If there is nothing broken, you will have it to-morrow.	Si no se rompió nada, lo tendrá V. mañana.
Don't forfeit your word.	No falte á su palabra.
You may rely on its being ready at that time.	V. puede contar que estará listo para ese tiempo.
Here are very beautiful clocks.	Aquí tiene V. hermosos relojes.
I want one.	Me falta uno.
You may choose.	Puede V. escojer.

Not to-day.	Hoy, no.
We will speak of it another time.	Hablarémos de eso otra vez.
Do you sell spectacles?	Vende V. anteojos?
I want an opera glass.	Necesito anteojos de teatro.
Do you keep microscopes?	Tiene V. microscópios?
This glass magnifies too much.	Este vidrio aumenta demasiado.
That does not magnify enough.	Ese no aumenta bastante.
That opera glass is good for nothing.	No valen nada esos gemelos.

To engage a Man-servant. — Para emplear un Criado.

Sir, I have heard you want a servant.	Señor, me dicen que V. necesita criado.
Yes; who has sent you to me?	Sí, quien le mandó aquí?
By whom are you recommended?	Por quien está V. recomendado?
By Mr. Butler, with whom I have travelled.	Por el Señor de Butler, con quien he viajado.
I know him very well.	Le conozco* muy bien.
On his recommendation, I shall not hesitate to take you into my service.	Bajo su recomendacion, no tengo inconveniente en tomarle á V. á mi servicio.
I suppose you possess the qualifications I want.	Supongo que V. tiene los requisitos necesários.

---

* *Conocer*, to know a person or a thing. *Saber*, to know about a person or thing. *Conozco* ese hombre, y *se* que no vendra: I know that man, and know he will not come.

TO ENGAGE A MAN-SERVANT.

shall stay in this town a fortnight longer.	Me quedo todavía quince dias en la villa.
Where have you travelled?	En donde ha viajado?
I have travelled in Germany and Italy.	He viajado por Alemánia é Italia.
Will you accompany me to Switzerland?	Quiére acompañarme á la Suécia?
I shall be a month on the road.	Estaré un mes de viage.
Have you performed that journey before?	Ha hecho V. ese viage ántes?
Sir, I am a Swiss.	Señor, soy Suizo.
How old are you?	Cuantos años tiene?
Are you a married man?	Es V. casado?
Were you long in Germany?	Estubo V. mucho tiempo en Alemánia?
Have you been long in France?	Hace mucho tiempo que está en Fráncia?
Can you ride on horseback?	Sabe V. montar á caballo?
Can you write?	Sabe escribir?
Yes, Sir.	Sí, Señor.
I understand German and Italian.	Entiendo el Aleman y el Italiano.
I likewise know the coins, weights and measures of the countries in which I have travelled.	Conozco tambien las monedas, los pesos y las medidas de los paises en que he viajado.
You may be very useful to me.	V. puede serme muy útil
What wages do you ask?	Que salario pide V.?
I have always had a	He tenido siempre cien

hundred dollars a year, and my board.	pesos al año, y la comida.
I will give you the same.	Le daré lo mismo.
I will give you fifteen dollars a month, but you will board yourself.	Le daré quince pesos al mes, no pagando su comida.
When we travel, I will pay your expenses.	Cuando* viajemos, yo pagaré sus gastos.
I must inform you that I will have no long bills.	Tengo que informarle que no quiero cuentas largas.
You must give me every evening an exact account of everything you have laid out for me.	Me dará todas las noches cuenta exacta de todo lo que ha gastado por mí.
I shall pay you immediately.	Le pagaré al instante.
I will call on your former master.	Pasaré á casa de su último amo.

To engage a Female Servant.

Para emplear una Criada.

Have you been long in service?	Hace mucho que sirve V.?
What is the last place you were at?	Como se llama su último amo?
Do you understand cookery?	Entiende V. de cocina?
Are you acquainted with the management of a house.	Entiende V. el gobierno doméstico?

* Cuando governs the subjunctive, when a future time is understood

TO ENGAGE A FEMALE SERVANT.

How old are you?	Que edad tiene V.?
You seem very young.	Parece V. muy jóven.
I am twenty-two.	Tengo veinte y dos años.
Do you understand needle-work?	Entiende de coser?
Are you a good seamstress?	Es V. buena costurera?
Can you wash fine linen?	Sabe V. lavar ropa fina?
Could you occasionally replace my waiting-woman?	Podria V. reemplazar de cuando en cuando á mi doncella?
Have you been in many families?	Ha servido V. en muchas familias?
Whose house have you left?	De que casa viene V. ahora?
Why did you leave your place?	Porqué dejó su empleo?
What can be the cause of your leaving?	Que fué la causa de su salida?
How long did you remain with her?	Cuanto tiempo estuvo V. con ella?
Will Mrs. L. give you a character?	La Señora L. le dará recomendacion?
I have a written character from Mrs. L.	Tengo recomendacion escrita de la Señora L.
Let me see it, I know her hand-writing.	Déjeme ver, conozco su escritura.
Do you like children?	Le gustan los niños?
What wages do you expect?	Que salario quiere V.?
Mrs. L. gave me fifty dollars.	La Señora de L. me daba* cincuenta pesos.

* In Spanish, the imperfect tense is used to imply custom, continuance of action, &c.

That is a great deal.	Eso es mucho.
But I think you will suit me.	Pero me parece que V. me convendrá.
I engage you from this moment.	Le tomo desde ahora mismo.
You may come to-morrow.	Puede V. venir mañana.

At a Shoemaker's. — En casa del Zapatero.

Have you shoes ready-made?	Tiene V. zapatos hechos?
Show me some of different sizes.	Enséñeme varios tamaños.
I will try these.	Probaré estos.
Give me the shoe horn.	Deme el calzador.
They hurt me.	Me lastiman.
I cannot walk.	No puedo andar.
They are too low.	Son demasiado bajos.
They are too high.	Son demasiado altos.
They are too large.	Son demasiado grandes.
They are too small.	Son demasiado pequeños.
The heels are too wide.	Los talones son demasiado anchos.
You had better take my measure.	Será mejor que V. me tome la medida.
Let me see some boots.	Enséñeme botas.
These are too narrow.	Estas son demasiado estrechas.
I think these will fit you well.	Creo que estas le vendrán á V bien.
The foot is narrow, but it will not hurt you.	El pié es estrecho, pero no le dañará á V.
In fact, they fit me very well.	De véras me estan muy bien.

Give me the boot-jack to pull them off.	Deme el tira-botas para quitarlas.
Make me also a pair of slippers.	Hágame tambien un par de pantuflos.
Of what colour?	De que color?
Make them very wide.	Hágamelos muy anchos.
Do not make the soles too thin.	No ponga V. suelas demasiado finas.
Take care that the binding be well sewed.	Cuidado que la bordura sea bien cosida.

With a Dressmaker. — Con una Modista.

Madam, I bring you your gowns.	Señora, le traigo á V. sus túnicos.
Ah! Miss A... is it you!	Ah! Señorita A... es V.!
I was impatient to see you.	Estaba impaciente por verla.
You have made me wait a long while.	V. me ha hecho esperar mucho.
How many dresses do you bring me?	Cuantos túnicos me trae V.?
Are they of different shapes?	Son de hechuras diferentes?
This dress fits me well.	Este túnico me viene bien.
This one appears very short.	Este me parece muy corto.
Morning gowns are now made so.	Las batas de mañana se usan así ahora.
I do not like them so short.	No me gustan tan cortas.
Let me try this.	Déjeme probar este.
Here is a French cambric dress to try on.	Aquí hay un túnico de batista para probar

Here is a muslin one, and a cambric muslin one.	Ahí tiene V. uno de muselina, y otra de muselina batista.
Take that pin out.	Quite ese alfiler.
Is all that sewed with care?	Todo está cosido con cuidado?
What trimmings will you put on this evening dress?	Que guarniciones va V. á poner á este vestido de paseo?
Is this trimming fashionable?	Es de moda, esta guarnicion?
They are much worn now.	Estan muy de moda ahora.
Is not this gown too full at the bottom?	¿No está este vestido muy ancho, de abajo?
I think it is; I can easily remedy it?	Creo que sí; pronto se remedia eso.
The sleeves are too tight.	Las mangas estan demasiado estrechas.
The sleeves are too wide.	Las mangas estan demasiado anchas.
The waist is too long.	La cintura está demasiado larga.
The waist is too short.	La cintura está demasiado estrecha.
The gown is not wide enough.	El túnico no es bastante ancho.
The plaits do not fall gracefully.	Los pliegues no caen con gracia.
The last fits the best.	El último me está lo mejor.
It fits my waist exactly.	Me viene justo en el pecho.
Take it for a pattern, and	Tome V. ese de muestra,

all the others will fit well,	y los demas me estaran bien.
Remember, I expect my things in a few days.	Acuérdese, espero todo dentro de pocos dias.
I will pay you when you bring everything you have to make for me.	Le pagaré cuando V. traiga todo lo que tiene que hacerme.
Be very punctual, I beg.	Tenga V. la bondad de ser exacta.
It is the only means of preserving my custom.	Es el solo modo de que yo le vuelva á comprar.
Madam, you shall have everything this morning.	Señora, tendrá V. todo, esta mañana.
You will oblige me.	V. me hará un favor.

To play at Chess. — Para jugar al Axedrez.

Let us play a game at chess.	Juguemos una partida de axedrez.
It is more amusing than whist, or even piquet.	Es mas divertido que *whist* ó *piquet*.
I do not know the game well.	No conozco bien el juego.
Where is the chess-board?	Endonde está el tablero?
Here it is with the chess men.	Aquí está, con las piezas.
Are our men arranged?	Estan puestas las piezas?
I want a bishop.	Me falta un alfil.
Your queen is not in its proper place.	Su reyna de V. no está en su lugar.
Who begins?	Quien es mano?
Let us draw.	Echemos suertes.
I have the first move.	Yo soy mano

It is a great advantage.	Es una gran ventaja.
I will forward this man.	Adelantaré esta pieza.
Your pieces are well supported.	Sus piezas de V. estan bien apoyadas.
I am afraid I must exchange pieces.	Temo verme en la necesidad de cambiar de piezas.
I have lost a knight.	He perdido un caballero.
I must castle.	Tengo que enrocar.
You cannot castle after having moved your king.	V. no puede enrocar, despues de haber mudado al rey.
Check to the king.	Jaque al rey.
I will cover this check with my castle.	Voy á cubrir ese jaque, con el roque.
I take it.	Lo tomo.
It is a drawn game.	Son tablas.
I was in hopes you would have given me checkmate.	Esperaba que V. me hubiera dado mate.
I cannot play with you.	No puedo jugar con V.
What odds will you give me?	Que ventaja me da V.
If you will give me a castle, I will try another game.	Si V. quiere darme un roque, probaré otra partida.
It is more than I ought, but I will do it with pleasure.	Es mas de lo que puedo dar, pero lo haré con gusto.

COLLECTION OF DETACHED SENTENCES.

COLECCION DE SENTÉNCIAS SUELTAS.

We translate English into French.	Traducimos el Ingles al Frances.
The study of languages is very useful.	El estudio de las lenguas es muy útil.
We intend to be very studious.	Vamos á ser muy estudiosos.
Come and see me this evening.	Venga á verme esta tarde.
He studies eight hours a day.	Estudia ocho horas al dia.
I sincerely congratulate you.	Le felicito sinceramente.
I love him much, for he is very attentive.	Le quiero mucho, por ser tan atento.
His memory is extraordinary.	Tiene una memoria extraordinaria.
My sister is still at a boarding-school.	Mi hermana está todavia de pupila.
We owe many obligations to your family.	Estamos muy obligados á la familia de V.
I will receive no excuses.	No recibo escusa ninguna.
I will come another day.	Vendré otro dia.
I have read sixteen pages this morning.	He leido esta mañana diez y seis páginas.
That edition is like the first.	Esa edicion es como la primera.
The new tragedy has succeeded.	La nueva trajedia ha salido bien.
Her voice is sweet, moving and melodious.	Tiene la voz dulce, patótica y harmoniosa.

I am taller and stronger than you.	Soy mas grande y mas fuerte que V.
This is the finest book in my library.	Es el libro mas hermoso de mi libreria.
The remedy is worse than the disease.	El remedio es peor que la enfermedad.
Your books are better bound than mine.	Sus libros de V. estan mejor encuadernados que los mios.
I do not know who has taken my grammar.	No sé quien ha llevado mi gramática.
Health is more precious than gold.	La salud es mas preciosa que el oro.
I rise at seven in the morning.	Me levanto á las siete.
My sister lives in France.	Mi hermana vive en Francia.
Young people are never satisfied.	Los jóvenes nunca estan contentos.
I call that a generous action.	Pues, es una accion generosa.
We do not remember it.	No nos acordamos de eso.
I, forget you! no, never!	¡Yo, olvidarte! no, nunca!
I know what you want.	Sé lo que V. necesita.
He is a literary man.	Es hombre de letras.
A great battle will be fought.	Se dará una batalla muy grande.
Has she not a bad cold?	No está muy constipada?
You forget an essential circumstance	V. olvida una circunstancia muy importante.
We set out to-morrow after breakfast.	Nos marchamos mañana, despues de almorzar.
I offer you my services	Le ofrezco á V. mis ser-

with all my heart.	vicios con todo mi corazon.
I perceive that they have deceived me.	Veo que me han engañado.
He expects company to-day.	Espera gente en casa, hoy.
It is during winter that poor people suffer most.	Padecen mas los pobres, en el invierno.
Will you go this evening to the play?	Quiere V. ir esta noche al teatro?
I do not think it will rain to-day.	No creo que llueva hoy.
I know that he is your friend.	Sé que es su amigo de V
Let us have something to eat immediately.	Dénos algo que comer, al instante.
When you are more attentive to my instructions, I will reward you.	Cuando pongas mas atencion a mis instrucciones, te recompensaré.
I shall return his visit to-day or to-morrow.	Pagaré su visita hoy o mañana.
If he has done that, I can do as much.	Si él hizo eso, puedo yo hacer otro tanto.
How do you find yourself this morning?	Como se halla V. esta mañana?
This is the finest village in the country.	Este pueblo es el mas bonito del pais.
I cannot believe a word of what he says.	No puedo creer una palabra de lo que dice.
Act with vigour, and you will succeed.	Obra con vigor y saldras bien.
will tell you what I think of it.	Yo le diré á V. mi parecer.

To whom are you now writing?	A quien está V. escribiendo?
I write to him every week.	Le escribo todas las semanas.
Politeness often proceeds from custom and experience.	La cortesía proviene muchas veces de la costumbre y de la esperiencia.
Nobody esteems you more than I do.	Nadie le aprecia á V. mas que yo.
The father and son died in the same year.	Muriéron el padre y el hijo, el mismo año.
I will give you ten guineas for it.	Le daré á V. diez guinéas.
I give him half-a-guinea a week.	Le doy media guinea cada semana.
I have spent a week in the country.	He pasado una semana en el campo.
What else can I do for you?	Que mas puedo hacer por V.?
Take this pen and give me the other.	Tome esta pluma, y deme la otra.
I wish you a good journey.	Buen viage.
That carpet is a very fine pattern.	Esa alfombra tiene un dibujo muy bonito.
Whose houses are those I see upon that hill?	De quien son esas casas que veo en aquella montaña?
That door does not shut well.	No cierra bien esa puerta.
We shall both go out after dinner.	Saldrémos los dos, despues de comer.
These young ladies are well brought up.	Estas señoritas son bien criadas

He is not as idle as his brother.	No es tan perezoso como su hermano.
He is the best of my friends.	Es el mejor de mis amigos.
If they are not ready, I will set out without them.	Si no estan listos, me marcho sin ellos.
I understand what you mean.	Entiendo lo que V. quiere decir.
I will never forget the favour you have done me.	No olvidaré nunca el favor que V. me ha hecho.
My brother is playing in the garden.	Mi hermano está jugando en la huerta.
We take a walk every day.	Nos paseamos todos los dias.
Pray send me your dictionary.	Hágame el favor de enviarme su diccionario.
He is a man of no learning.	Es hombre sin educacion ninguna.
Certainly we are mistaken.	Es claro que nos engañamos.
I did not know you then.	No le conocia á V. entónces.
I have almost done.	He casi acabado.
You play a great deal too much.	Juegas demasiado.
With your leave.	Con el permiso de V.
She is incapable of falsehood.	No es capaz de mentira.
Shall I speak ingenuously to you?	Quiere V. que le hable con franqueza?
I have no answer to give you.	No puedo contestarle.

By studying attentively you will make rapid progress.	A fuerza de estudiar atentamente, adelantará V mucho.
How troublesome you are!	¡Que molesto es V.!
He studies natural philosophy.	Está estudiando la filosofia natural.
Our lessons seem to be very difficult.	Nuestras lecciones parecen muy difíciles.
We are satisfied with his conduct.	Estamos satisfechos de su conducta
I am myself of that opinion.	Yo tambien mantengo esa opinion.
What does your friend say?	¿Que dice su amigo?
Pope was an Englishman.	Pope era Ingles.
Bring the table nearer.	Acerque V. la mesa.
His protection has been very useful to me.	Su proteccion me ha sido muy útil.
That knife is yours.	Ese cuchillo es de V.
I have said nothing that could offend you.	No he dicho nada que deba ofenderle.
A great misfortune has happened.	Ha sucedido una grande desdicha.
Think of what you have to do.	Piense V. en lo que tiene que hacer.
Do not forget to carry that letter to the post-office.	No olvide V. llevar esa carta al correo.
I have no time to lose.	No tengo tiempo que perder.
Have you finished your exercise?	Ha acabado V. su tema?
Yes, I have.	Sí, Señor.
We drank your health.	Hemos bebido á la salud de V.

Go and fetch me the atlas.	Vete á buscar el Átlas.
She is as pale as death.	Está pálida como la muerte.
We were very unhappy.	Eramos muy infelices.
What is your intention?	Quo piensa V. hacer?
The work is in twenty-five volumes.	Es una obra en veinte y cinco tomos.
Those events will be fatal to your country.	Esos sucesos seran fatales á su pais de V.
I have read this book from the beginning to the end.	He leido este libro del principio al fin.
Paternal authority is the first and most respectable of all laws.	La autoridad paternal es la primera y la mas respetable de todas las leyes.
What are you thinking of?	En que está V. pensando?
Did they not speak too much?	No habláron demasiado?
We never walk in the evening.	Nunca nos paseamos por la tarde.
What a beautiful girl!	¡Que hermosa muchacha!
She is very much altered in her conduct.	Ha mudado mucho de conducta.
She is very much altered since her illness.	Se ha descompuesto mucho desde su enfermedad.
Did not your dog bite everybody?	Su perro no mordia a todo el mundo?
I was going to your house when I met you.	Iba á su casa cuando lo encontré.
You had foretold that event.	V. habia predicho ese evento.
This street is too noisy for	Esta calle es demasiado

those who love retirement and study.	ruidosa para aquellos que gustan del retiro y del estudio.
Shall I suffer patiently such an insult?	Sufriré con paciencia un insulto semejante?
If your book is not upon the table, perhaps it is under it.	Si tu libro no está encima, acaso estará debajo de la mesa.
How many leaves have you read?	Cuantas hojas ha leido V.?
We expect him every minute.	Le esperamos á cada instante.
I am determined to stay at home.	He determinado quedarme en casa.
I forbid you expressly to go with him.	Te prohibo espresamente ir con él.
How far do you intend to take us?	Hasta donde quiere V conducirnos?
I will do it, since you wish it.	Pues V. lo quiere, lo haré.
You know better than anybody, that merit is not always rewarded.	V. sabe mejor que ninguno, que el mérito no tiene siempre su premio.
The Danube is the largest river in Europe.	El Danubio es el rio mas grande de Europa.
They seldom go out.	Salen rara vez.
We fear we shall not succeed	Tememos que nos salga mal.
I love him as my son.	Le quiero como á mi hijo.
No man can please him.	Nadie le puede agradar.
What reproaches can you make me?	Que reconvenciones me puede V. hacer?

Where are you going so early?	A donde va V. tan temprano?
I shall not conceal from you my mind.	No le ocultaré á V. mi modo de pensar.
Does she acknowledge her error.	Reconoce su error?
I did make use of his book, but I did not tear it.	Me he servido de su libro, mas no lo rompí.
This is for you, and that is for me.	Esto es para V. y eso para mí.
It begins to be very warm.	Ya se pone caliente.
He was elected by a great majority.	Fué elejido por una pluralidad muy grande.
He runs faster than I.	Corre mas que yo.
I do not know how to remunerate you.	No sé como recompensarle á V.
I sent for the physician.	Envié buscar al médico.
He never answers but yes or no.	Nunca contesta mas que sí ó no.
You pay little attention to what I tell you.	Haces poco caso de lo que te digo.
Every one relates that story differently.	Cada uno lo cuenta de un modo diferente.
As soon as he received the news, he set off.	Al instante que recibió la noticia, se fué.
I have the head-ache.	Tengo dolor de cabeza
I do not know what books you wish to read.	No sé que libros quiere V leer.
This is my opinion; what is yours?	Esa es mi opinion, ¿que le parece á V.?
The French revolution lasted six and twenty years.	La revolucion Francesa duró veinte y seis años

His room is above mine.	Su cuarto está encima del mio.
He is fit for anything.	Es bueno para todo.
He never has money.	Nunca tiene dinero.
I was in Paris two years ago.	Estaba en Paris, hace dos años.
Do your exercise before it is too late.	Haz tu tema ántes que sea demasiado tarde.
They will bring a charge against you.	Presentaran un cargo contra V.
We met at your uncle's.	Nos vímos en casa de su tio.
I forgive you, because I hope you will behave better for the future.	Te perdono, porque creo que te conduciras mejor en adelante.
I am no longer angry with him.	Ya no estoy enfadado con él
Tell me what I can do for you.	Dígame lo que puedo hacer por V.
Time passes away rapidly; it is five already.	¡Pronto pasa el tiempo! ya son las cinco.
Your father will certainly arrive to-morrow.	Seguramente llegará su padre de V. mañana
Without application it is impossible to succeed.	Sin aplicarse, es imposible adelantar.
This will certainly displease your father.	Seguramente esto ofenderá a tu padre.
I assure you I will write to-morrow, if possible.	Le aseguro á V. que, siendo posible, escribo mañana.
We intend to go to London next week.	Hemos convenido en ir á Lóndres la semana que viene.
Could you not find that	No ha podido V. encon-

word in your dictionary?	trar esa palabra en su diccionario.
She is respected by all those who know her.	Es respetada de todos los que la conocen.
This is a well-written composition.	Es una composicion muy bien escrita
The opportunity is entirely lost.	Se perdió enteramente la ocasion
I am often interrupted by troublesome people.	A cada rato me interrumpen algunos importunos.
I came in at the moment you were going out.	Entraba cuando V. salia.
He has made a present to his sister.	Ha hecho un regalo á su hermana.
I will do it willingly, if you wish.	Lo haré con gusto, si V. quiere.
We set out together, but we parted the next day.	Salímos juntos, pero nos separámos al dia siguiente.
Now as it is fine weather, let us take a walk.	Ahora que hace buen tiempo, vamos á pasear.
How much does that carriage cost you?	Cuanto le cuesta ese quitrin?
I cannot do that exercise without your assistance.	No puedo hacer ese tema sin la ayuda de V.
She has done it on purpose.	Lo hizo á propósito.
What does he complain of?	De que se queja?
Stay with me till the rain be over.	Quédese V. conmigo hasta que cese la lluvia
If you want paper, here is some.	Aquí hay papel, si V quiere.
I don't want any.	No necesito.

Let him set out immediately.	Que se vaya al instante
She is incapable of attention.	No es capaz de atencion
That reason is the best you can give.	Es la mejor razon que V puede dar.
Do you follow me so everywhere?	Me sigues así por todas partes?
The event is doubtful; at least I fear so.	El evento es dudoso; á lo ménos lo creo.
Will not your sister come before six o'clock?	No vendrá su hermana ántes de las seis?
He is shorter by an inch.	Es una pulgada mas corto.
We are in the depth of winter.	Estamos en medio del invierno.
We will see you home, if you allow us.	Con el permiso de V., vamos á acompañarle á casa.
I am surprised at his impudence.	Me sorprende mucho su insolencia.
Why do you not open the windows?	Porqué no abre V. las ventanas?
They are not pleased with his conduct	No les gusta su conducta.
You will hurt him more than you think.	V. le hará mas daño de lo que piensa.
We are going to meet him.	Vamos á encontrarle.
That will never happen.	Eso no sucederá nunca.
His countenance inspires terror.	Su cara da miedo.
Give him a reward for his good conduct.	Recompénsele V. por su buena conducta.
The morning is the proper time for study.	La mañana es el mejor tiempo para estudiar.

It is the opinion of some writers.	Es la opinion de algunos autores.
Have you no answer to give me?	No puedes contestarme?
The whole fleet is at sea.	La flota está toda en el mar.
Cast your eyes on the other side of the river.	Mire V. al otro lado del rio.
Tell me which of those ladies pleases you most.	Dígame cual de esas damas le gusta mas.
That chain is not gold, it is gilt.	Esa cadena no es de oro es dorada.
He is not ashamed of his conduct.	No se avergüenza de su conducta.
I was not ill, yet I was not well.	No estaba ni malo ni bueno.
Were you not in the wrong?	V. no se ha equivocado?
I will explain that passage to you.	Le expliquaré á V. ese pasage.
You had money yesterday; have you any now?	V. tenia dinero ayer; ¿tiene V. hoy?
I was by him when the accident happened.	Estaba á su lado, cuando le sucedió el accidente.
I shall give him my note.	Le daré mi nota (mi pagaré).
Let them employ their time well.	Que empléen bien su tiempo.
There must be an error somewhere.	Habrá equivocacion por alguna parte.
Is your master pleased with you?	Tu maestro está contento contigo?
He will never pardon him.	No le perdonará nunca.

What! your shoes are already worn out!	¡Que! estan ya viejos tus zapatos!
I saw him at New-York this day week.	Le ví en Nueva York, hoy hace ocho dias.
What is your name?	Como se llama V.?
My name is George.	Me llamo Jorge.
I have so much to do, that I have not a moment to lose.	Tengo tanto que hacer, que no puedo perder un instante.
His behaviour does not please me.	Su conducta no me gusta.
Why do you prevent that child from studying his lesson?	Porqué no dejas ese niño que estudie su leccion?
Have you learned your phrases?	Has aprendido tus frases?
If you feel indisposed, go to bed.	Si te sientes indispuesto, vete á la cama.
I give him the fifth part of my income.	Le doy la quinta parte de mis rentas.
He is not as rich as he is said to be.	No es tan rico como se ha creido.
I would write better if I had not such a bad pen.	Escribiria mejor si no tuviera tan mala pluma.
Why do they go away so soon?	Porqué se van tan temprano?
Playing is his principal occupation.	Se ocupa principalmente en jugar.
They were beginning to read when he came in.	Ya estaban leyendo cuando entró.
Let us rest here for half-an hour.	Descansemos aquí média hora.
I am afraid they will be expelled	Temo que sean espulsados.

Pray do it as soon as possible.	Hágame V. el favor de hacerlo lo mas pronto posible.
They accepted my offer and the affair was settled.	Aceptáron mi oferta, y se cerró el negocio.
We cannot always play; we must study likewise.	No podemos siempre jugar; es preciso tambien estudiar.
He is awkward in everything he does.	No tiene maña para hacer nada.
I did not think she could walk so far.	No creia que ella pudiese caminar tanto.
Though he says so, nobody believes him.	Aunque lo diga, nadie le cree.
We will not breakfast without you.	No almorzarémos sin V.
She will not interfere in that business.	No se mezclará en ese negocio.
I fear she told a story to excuse herself.	Temo que haya dicho una mentira para escusarse.
We were covered with dust.	Estábamos cubiertos de polvo.
Will you go to France this summer?	Irá V. á Francia este verano?
I did not think he would go away so soon.	No creia que se marchase tan temprano.
Is not the servant waiting for an answer?	No está el criado esperando la respuesta?
I heard she was very rich.	He oido decir que estaba muy rica.
Do not make rash vows.	No haga V. votos precipitados.
I met him about dusk.	Le encontré al anochecer

He has been the maker of his own fortune.	El solo ha hecho su fortuna.
Indeed, said she, that is what I will never do.	De véras, dijo ella, eso es lo que no haré nunca.
He is a very agreeable man in society.	Es un hombre muy agradable en su conversacion.
We have dined very early to-day.	Hemos comido muy temprano hoy.
To-morrow I set out for Holland.	Mañana me marcho para Holanda.
I shall easily convince you of this truth.	Le convenceré facilmente de esa verdad.
He and she did the whole work.	El y ella hiciéron todo el trabajo.
Eat one of these apples.	Coma V. una de estas manzanas.
Congress will meet on the fourth of next month.	El Congreso se reunirá el cuatro del mes que viene.
It is difficult to land on that coast.	Es difícil desembarcar en esa costa.
He is a man of common abilities.	Es hombre de poco talento.
The greater part of the members rose.	La mayor parte de los miembros se levantáron.
I have not heard from you for a long while	Hace mucho tiempo que no he recibido noticias de V.
He met him in the street and brought him to his house.	Le encontró en la calle, y le llevó á su casa.
She had a moderate understanding.	Tenia un entendimiento regular.

I have spoken to my brother of all that happened.	He hablado con mi hermano de todo lo que sucedió.
Upon the whole, I like him well enough.	Con todo, me gusta bastante.
My sister lives en France	Mi hermana vive en Francia.
Experience confirms my opinion.	La esperiencia confirma mi opinion.
Italy is a beautiful country.	La Italia es país muy hermoso.
His father is an officer of great merit.	Su padre es oficial de mucho mérito.
A sad accident has befallen me.	Me ha sucedido una desgracia.
He is a middle-aged man.	Es hombre de mediana edad.
I perceive that I have required too much of you.	Veo que le he exigido demasiado.
What you tell me is incredible.	Lo que V. me dice es increible.
They fear she will become blind.	Temen que se vuelva ciega.
Why do you give me the trouble of doing it?	Porqué me da V. el trabajo de hacerlo?
Did you find the letter you had lost?	Encontró V. la carta que habia perdido?
There is no danger in crossing the river.	No hay peligro en pasar el rio.
She is prodigal to excess.	Es escesivamente pródiga.
I not only paid him, but even made him a present.	No solamente le pagué pero le hice un regalo

From what you say, we must believe it.	Segun lo que V dice, tenemos que creerlo.
So you saw him, and spoke to him.	Pues V. le vió y le habló.
Such a fault deserves punishment.	Culpa semejante merece castigo.
Come as often as you can.	Venga V. lo mas amenudo posible.
In winter, the roads are always worse than in summer.	En el invierno los caminos estan siempre peores que en el verano.
When do you intend to do your exercise?	Cuando piénsas hacer tu tema?
This house is well situated.	Esta casa está muy bien situada.
I have a mind to speak to your sister.	Tengo gana de hablar con su hermana de V.
I am more than half convinced.	Estoy mas que médio convencido.
I have not slept two hours the whole night.	No he dormido dos horas en toda la noche.
Shall we not take our usual walk before breakfast?	No vamos á dar el paseo acostumbrado ántes de almorzar.?
In the full vigour of life.	En el vigor de su edad
Is the chamber-door shut?	Está cerrada la puerta del cuarto?
Will you give me that proof of friendship?	Me dará V esa prueba de su amistad?
We have heard from our brother.	Hémos tenido noticias de nuestro hermano.
We had just arrived when he came in.	Acababamos de llegar cuando él entró.
To be about a thing.	Estar haciendo una cosa

He and I learn French.	El é yo estudiamos el Frances.
We have a fine country-house and a spacious garden.	Tenemos una hermosa casa de campo, y una huerta espaciosa.
How elegant and instructive are the works of Fenelon!	¡Cuan elegantes é instructivas son las obras de Fenelon!
This story is very entertaining.	Este cuento es muy divertido.
How many children has he?	¿Cuantos niños tiene?
Believe me, he is an honest man, I answer for his probity.	Créeme, es hombre honrado, respondo de su honradez.
His small income affords him all the comforts of life.	Sus pequeñas rentas le proporcionan las comodidades de la vida.
He is the most covetous man I know.	Es el hombre mas codicioso que conozco.
Everybody knows it except you.	Todos lo saben sino V.
He will come this day three weeks.	Vendrá de hoy en tres semanas.
Nothing would deter him from it.	Nada le privaria de hacerlo.
I have been here above an hour	Hace mas de media hora que estoy aquí.
He was beaten, strong as he is.	Por mas fuerte que es, no dejó de ser vencido.
Give me my book. I want it.	Dame mi libro, lo necesito.
They are going to take an airing in the carriage.	Van á pasear en el quitrin.

I returned him a polite answer.	Le dí una respuesta política.
When I have lost something, I look for it.	Cuando pierdo algo, lo busco.
Most romances spoil the judgment.	La mayor parte de los romances confunden el entendimiento.
Your friend is in distress; think of him.	Su amigo de V. está afligido; acuérdese V. de él.
I have been up these two hours.	Me levanté, hace dos horas.
We have received a letter this morning.	Recibímos carta esta mañana.
He pays unusual attention to her advice.	Hace mucho caso de sus consejos.
That would suit me very well.	Eso me convendria muy bien.
He wants to know everything.	Quiere saber todo
I am very glad you are well.	Me alegro que V. esté bueno.
The more you speak to your brother, the less he minds your advice.	Tanto mas hablas á tu hermano, tanto ménos se acuerda de tus consejos.
He will lend you money, since he promised it.	Le prestará á V. dinero, pues lo ha prometido.
Is your mother in the country?	Su madre de V. está en el campo?
She is as fine a girl as any I ever saw.	Muchacha mas linda nunca la he visto.
His looks betrayed his sentiments.	Sus ojos hiciéron traicion á su corazon

I have no personal acquaintance with those ladies.	No conozco personalmente á esas Señoras.
That trimming suits the gown.	Esa guarnicion sienta bien al túnico.
You take a great deal of pains.	V. pone mucho cuidado.
Is she not an accomplished young lady?	No es una Señorita muy bien instruida?
Is your father in his study?	Tu padre está en el gabinete?
Your mamma will be very much pleased.	Tu madre estará muy contenta.
It is full three years since he left his family.	Ya hace mas de tres años que dejó á su familia.
He has spent a great deal of money in his travels.	Ha gastado mucho dinero en sus viages.
A man of general acquaintance.	Un hombre generalmente instruido.
Do me the pleasure to mention it to him.	Hágame V. el favor de decirle.
You show too much animosity against him.	V le demuestra demasiada enemistad.
I never saw a more modest young man.	Nunca he visto á jóven mas contenido.
He has reached an honourable old age.	Ha llegado á una honrosa vejez.
I am really surprised that you should express such a sentiment.	Realmente me sorprende que V. se espresa en esos términos.
He went away without saying a word.	Se marchó sin decir nada
Did you come by yourself?	V. vino solo?

17

This word is very hard to pronounce.	Es muy difícil pronunciar esta palabra.
She is overwhelmed with grief.	Está anonadada de dolor
I would rather have the word of an honest man than his oath.	Tomaria mejor la palabra que el juramento de un hombre honrado.
We trespass on your goodness.	Abusamos de su bondad de V.
Can you clear yourself of that charge?	Puede V. defenderse de esa acusacion?
There are striking beauties in that new poem.	Hay grandes bellezas en ese poema nuevo.
He will not come unless they send for him.	No vendrá, á ménos que le manden buscar.
He did it with astonishing courage.	Lo hizo con un valor admirable.
He has much improved in politeness.	Ha mejorado mucho su educacion.
She is not dumb I assure you.	Le aseguro á V. que no es muda.
He stammers	Tartamudea.
His life has been a mixture of adversity and prosperity.	Su vida ha sido una mezcla de desgracias y prosperidades.
They look upon his death as unavoidable.	Miran su muerte como inevitable.
I have not succeeded in my undertaking.	Mi empresa me ha salido mal.
Well, Sir, shall we have the honour of seeing you in a few days?	Señor, tendrémos el honor de verle á V. dentro de pocos dias?
I never saw a more despicable man.	Nunca he visto hombre mas despreciable.

Your honour is concerned.	Su honor está por medio
Reading is very useful to young people.	La lectura es muy útil á los jóvenes.
She has been dead these three years.	Hace tres años que murió.
I could not remain in so unwholesome a climate.	No podia quedarme en un pais tan enfermizo.
I paid little attention to his discourse.	Hice poco caso de su discurso.
I beg you to speak to my cousin.	Le suplico á V. que hable con mi primo.
Bid him come, we have something to give him	Dígale que venga, tenemos algo que darle.
I am very sorry to hear she is so ill.	Siento mucho que esté mala.
Who is that gentleman?	Quien es ese Señor?
He will soon publish a new edition of his work.	En poco tiempo publicará otra edicion de su obra.
This hat is the gentleman's.	Este es el sombrero del Señor.
She received me kindly.	Me recibió con urbanidad.
I shall be glad of your acquaintance.	Tendré mucho gusto en conocerle á V.
He behaves better than he did before.	Se conduce mejor que ántes.
I will go and pay my duty to her.	Voy á cumplir con ella.
What lady did you see at Mrs. D...'s?	Que Señora vió V. en casa de la Señora D...?
What is the name of this red flower?	Como se llama esta flor encarnada?
Do you think of me?	Piensa V. en mí?
Yes, I do.	Sí, de véras.
Put down the blinds.	Baje las persianas.

This young gentleman is too grave for his age.	Este Señorito es demasiado sério para su edad.
Take care not to overset the chairs.	Cuidado de no volcar las sillas.
He pays his addresses to that lady.	Está cortejando á esa Señorita.
Of all things in the world, history is the most enlightening.	De todas las cosas del mundo, la historia es la mas instructiva.
He is continually running from street to street.	Corre continuamente de calle en calle.
Don't they come and see him now and then?	No le vienen á ver de cuando en cuando?
Is this your way of proceeding?	Es ese su modo de obrar?
He did all that he could to hurt me.	Hizo todo lo posible para hacerme daño.
He is a man of decided character.	Es hombre de un carácter firme.
His manner of relating the different adventures of his travels, pleased me extremely.	Su modo de referir las aventuras diferentes de su viage, me gustó muchísimo.
How many times a week does your master attend you?	·Cuantas veces cada semana viene tu maestro?
I see we shall be good friends to-day.	Veo que estarémos amigos hoy.
I should displease all my family.	Disgustaria á toda mi familia.
I have very weak eyes.	Tengo los ojos muy débiles.
She has married a perfect gentleman.	Se casó con todo un caballero.

never heard so much nonsense.	Nunca he oido tanta jerigonza.
He has given me a thousand proofs of his friendship.	Me ha dado mil pruebas de su amistad.
I will profit by the information you give me.	Me aprovecharé de los informes que V. me da.
He has neglected to send me his direction.	Descuidó darme su direccion.
Tell her I never will forget her kindness.	Dígale V. que nunca olvidaré su bondad.
Everybody esteems him for his ingenuousness.	Todos le estiman por su candor.
What are these men doing?	Que hacen aquellos hombres?
We are engaged for tomorrow night.	Estámos comprometidos para mañana á noche.
Have you any money to lend me?	Tiene V. dinero que prestarme?
We want three hundred dollars.	Necesitamos tres cientos duros.
Never read frivolous or dangerous books.	No leas nunca libros frívolos ó peligrosos.
He always interrupts me when I am speaking.	Me interrumpe siempre cuando estoy hablando.
You propose the best advice.	V. propone el mejor consejo.
My dear Caroline, I see you improve every day.	Cara Carolina mia, veo que adelantas todos los dias.
She lives hard by, opposite the City Hall.	Vive muy cerca de aquí, en frente de la Intendéncia.
Where is the post-office?	Endonde está el Correo?

The study of languages is very entertaining.	Es muy divertido el estudio de las lenguas.
I beg to be excused.	Le suplico á V. que me perdone.
Excuse me for not having come.	Perdóneme el no haber venido.
I now find it less beautiful than when I bought it.	Me parece ménos hermoso, que cuando lo compré.
I am going to spend a fortnight with my friend B...	Voy á pasar quince dias con mi amigo B..
Shall I offer you some chicken?	Gusta V. tomar un pedacito de pollo?
I arrived at three in the afternoon.	Llegué á las tres de la tarde.
She draws advantage from everything.	Saca ventaja de todo.
She is still more covetous than her husband.	Es todavía mas avara que su marido.
I will never believe so incredible a thing.	Jamas daré asenso á cosa tan increible.
It is incredible how many works that author has composed.	Es increible el número de obras que ha escrito ese autor.
He is without friends, because he speaks with insolence to everybody.	Se encuentra sin amigos, porque habla con insolencia á todo el mundo.
You have neglected your dress this morning.	V. ha descuidado vestirse esta mañana.
We expected a more civil answer.	Esperábamos una respuesta mas política.
A person rather advanced in age	Una persona mas bien entrada en años.

They improve very much.	Hacen muchos progresos.
She wears a straw hat with a white ribbon.	Trae sombrero de paja con cinta blanca.
This is of no advantage to me.	Esto no me aprovecha nada.
They praised you very highly.	Encomiáron á V.
Favour me with your direction.	Hágame V. el favor de darme el número de su casa
We invited him to dine and to sup with us.	Le convidámos á comer y cenar con nosotros.
He pleases everybody by his open and frank behaviour.	Agrada á todo el mundo por su comportamiento lleno de franqueza y afabilidad.
She has a more melodious voice than her sister.	Tiene una voz mas melodiosa que su hermana.
I have exchanged my carriage for a more convenient one.	He cambiado mi carruage por otro mas cómodo.
I wish you a speedy return.	Deseo que V. vuelva pronto.
All that is nothing but a joke.	Todo eso es bromá
He has been blind these three years	Hace tres años que esta ciego.
He likes better to walk than to work.	Mas le gusta caminar que trabajar.
You don't know how amiable she is.	No sabe V. cuan amable es.
That is natural at his age.	Es muy natural á su edad
Do not trouble me any more.	No vuelva V. á molestarme.

She diverts herself with playing on the piano and singing.	Se divierte en tocar el piano y cantar.
Does not that satisfy you?	No se contenta V. con eso?
It is a very foolish undertaking.	Es una empresa muy tonta.
How peacefully he sleeps! don't wake him.	¡Que apaciblemente duerme! no le despierte V.
The style of that author is more grammatical than elegant.	El estilo de ese autor es mas gramatical que elegante.
If it had not been for you I would have punished him.	Si no fuera por V. le habria castigado.
At least do not dismiss him.	A lo ménos no le despida V.
There were too many people in the room.	Habia demasiada gente en el cuarto.
After all, what shall we do?	Pues, ¿que hay que hacer?
She has as much good sense as experience.	Tiene tanto juicio como esperiencia.
I beseech you do not abandon me.	Le suplico á V. que no me abandone.
This canal is not yet navigable.	Este canal todavía no está navegable.
Their parting was affecting.	Su separacion fué muy penosa.
There was nobody but the master.	No habia nadie sino el maestro.
I found it agreed very well with me.	Hallaba que me convenia perfectamente.
She grieves at everything.	Todo le aflije

My horse fell under me.	Mi caballo cayó debajo de mí.
Do not believe she has done it on purpose.	No crea V. que lo hizo á propósito.
As to you, you may do as you please.	En cuanto á V., puede hacer como guste.
I did not write, for want of an opportunity.	No he escrito, por falta de ocasion.
These trees are too much exposed to the wind.	Estos árboles estan demasiado espuestos al viento.
I took a walk along the sea-shore.	He dado un paseo por la orilla del mar.
She is not so old as I thought.	Es mas jóven de lo que creia.
Once more, I comprehend nothing of all this.	Otra vez, no entiendo nada de eso.
It is easily seen that you are a foreigner.	Se ve al instante que V. es estrangero.
Repeat your last lesson	Repite tu última leccion,
He is gone to his country-house.	Se fué á su casa de campo.
They are free from affectation.	No son afectadas.
He has as many friends as anybody.	Tiene tantos amigos como cualquiera.
I shall go out in half-an-hour.	Saldré dentro de media hora.
Give my love to your sister.	Memorias á tu hermana.
This letter is to be sent post-paid.	Es preciso pagar el porte de esta carta.
I will frank it if you please.	La franquearé, si V. gusta

He did it without telling it to him.	Lo hizo sin decirle nada.
Speak to him, he is inclined to serve you.	Háblele V., está listo para servirle.
At that time I was fond of travelling.	En ese tiempo me gustaba viajar.
When my mother died she was forty-four years of age.	Mi madre tenia cuarenta y cuatro años cuando murió.
As we have several places to call at, we must set out early.	Como tenemos que hacer muchas visitas, debemos de salir temprano
He made them all sit down at table.	Les mandó á todos sentarse á la mesa.
May you live happy!	¡Que V. viva feliz!
If you continue to study four hours a day, you will become learned.	Si estúdias cuatro horas cada dia, llegaras á ser un sabio.
Walking is a great enjoyment in the spring.	El paseo es muy agradable en la primavera.
I do not reject your kind offers.	No desprecio sus buenas ofertas.
They speak to me, as well as to you and to them.	Me hablan á mí, tan bien como á V. y á ellos.
What was he doing when you saw him?	Que estaba haciendo cuando V. le vió?
They insulted him publicly.	Le insultáron en público.
She has taken a great dislike to her.	Le ha cojido odio.
I take it at your word.	Lo tomo bajo su garantia
This letter is directed to you.	Esta carta está dirijida á V.
Their hatred and their	Su odio y su animosidad

animosity will wear off in time.	pasaran con el tiempo
Do not be uneasy, all will be right.	No tenga V. cuidado todo irá bien
The footman has not yet found a place.	El lacayo todavía no ha encontrado colocacion.
He is reduced to the utmost extremity.	Está reducido á la última miseria.
I pronounce well, don't I?	Pronuncio bien, ¿ es verdad ?
It would be polite in you to wait upon him.	Seria de V. un acto de urbanidad pasar á verle.
His progress is slow, but solid.	Sus progresos no son grandes, pero sólidos.
That action does not deserve a better reward.	Esa accion no merece mejor recompensa.
His misfortunes have soured his temper.	Sus desgracias han agriado su temperamento.
I shall mention that event.	Mencionaré esa casualidad.
I have not abandoned my friend.	No he abandonado á mi amigo,
My brother and sister have caught cold.	Mi hermano y mi hermana han cojido frio.
I cannot afford to spend so much.	No tengo los medios necesarios para gastar tanto.
Remember me to him.	Dele memorias de mi parte.
My sister begs to be remembered to you.	Mi hermana dice que no se olvida de V.
I was speaking of him when he came in.	Estaba hablando de él cuando entró.
The rose is more beautiful than the violet.	La rosa es mas bella que la violeta

I give you these books, but do not lend them to your brother.	Te doy estos libros, pero no los prestes á tu hermano.
Reading is to the mind, what eating and drinking are to the body.	La lectura es al alma, como el comer y beber al cuerpo.
They will be very much fatigued by so long a walk.	Estaran muy cansados de paseo tan largo.
He supported his opinion by several authorities.	Apoyó su opinion en várias autoridades.
His friend received him with open arms.	Su amigo le recibió con los brazos abiertos.
I know my opinion will not be agreeable.	Sé que mi opinion no le será agradable.
I thank you for your kind inquiries.	Le doy á V. las gracias por el interes que V se toma.
Will Mr. H ... suffer an insult; he, who is so proud?	Sufrirá el Señor H... un insulto? él, que es tan orgulloso?
Born and brought up in adversity.	Nacido y criado en adversidad.
My brother and sister caught cold last night in the garden.	Mi hermano y mi hermana cojiéron frio ayer á noche en la huerta.
He has given up his design.	Ha abandonado su proyecto.
I confess it to my shame.	Lo confieso, a mi ver güenza.
I keep up a regular correspondence with him.	Mantengo una correspondencia regular con él.
The more you apply yourself, the more you learn.	Tanto mas V. se aplique, mas aprenderá.

That man has much cleverness, but he has no learning.	Ese hombre tiene mucho conocimiento, pero poca sabiduria.
Send it, if you please, by the first opportunity.	Hágame V. el favor de enviarlo la primera ocasion.
Tell me sincerely, would you do it?	Dígame, de véras, ¿ lo haria V. ?
It is a great comfort to have such children.	Es un gran consuelo tener niños semejantes.
I spend my time in reading and writing.	Paso el tiempo en leer y escribir.
Let us make haste and dress.	Vámos; vistámonos pronto
If they ask you a favour will you refuse it to them?	Si le piden un favor, rehusará V. ?
I have to do with civil people.	Yo tengo que tratar con gente civilizada.
That man is extremely learned.	Ese hombre es muy sabio.
There is no such a word in the language.	No hay tal palabra en la lengua.
They passed the whole day in the fields.	Pasáron el dia entero en los campos.
I will come once a week; is that too often?	Vendré una vez cada semana; ¿ es demasiado amenudo ?
You proposed a very dangerous project.	V. ha propuesto un proyecto muy peligroso.
I shall not trust you any longer with my secrets.	No le fiaré á V. mas mis secretos.
She has a very pleasing countenance	Tiene una cara muy agradable

18

I could not help it.	No era culpa mia.
He is a naughty boy.	Es muy mal muchacho.
I know them both, I will employ them.	Los conozco á los dos, les daré empleo.
How can you have so much credulity.	Como puede V. ser tan crédulo ?
We are ready to do whatever you may think proper.	Estamos listos para hacer todo lo que V. quiera
I should do a great injustice.	Haria una grande injusticia.
We have never suspected his probity.	Nunca hémos sospechado de su probidad.
He has a country-way about him.	Tiene modales rústicos
She is unworthy of your friendship.	No es digna de su amistad.
I always thought he was unworthy of her.	Le creia siempre indigno de ella
There is something graceful in this picture.	Hay algo de grácia en esa pintura.
That passage alludes to an old story.	Ese pasage alude á una historia antigua.
I fear I shall not be able to do it.	Temo no poder hacerlo.
He has lost all the esteem he had for her.	Ha perdido la estimacion en que la tenia.
His reasoning is not better than yours.	Su modo de raciocinar no es mejor que él de V.
My servant came back on foot.	Volvió á pié mi criado.
You shall answer for his conduct.	V. responderá de su conducta.
That exceeds all belief.	Eso no se puede creer

DETACHED SENTENCES.

He knows a little of everything.	Sabe un poço de todo.
She becomes less and less supportable.	Se vuelve mas y mas insoportable.
I never met him since.	No le he encontrado despues.
Come, at the latest, at eleven o'clock.	Venga á las once, lo mas tarde.
Do them that pleasure, if you can.	Hágales V. ese favor, si es posible.
He has given me several proofs of friendship.	Me ha dado bastantes pruebas de amistad.
We have sent for the surgeon.	Hemos mandado buscar al cirujano.
He did it, and even boasts of it.	Lo hizo, y aun se vanagloria de haberlo hecho.
He has all the comforts of life.	Tiene todas las comodidades de la vida.
She is not pleased with her maid.	No está contenta de su criada.
Carry all that up stairs.	Lleve todo eso arriba.
We dread fatigue more than danger.	Tememos mas la fatiga que el peligro.
We lead a very quiet life.	Pasamos una vida muy tranquila.
She is never tired of reading novels.	Nunca se cansa de leer novelas.
His mother was then thirty years old.	Entonces, tenia su madre treinta años.
I wish to resume French.	Quiero repasar el Frances
He has not lost his senses	No ha perdido el juicio
You seem to have made it a point to contradict me	Parece que su mayor gusto es contradecirme

At how much do you value that horse?	En cuanto valua V. ese caballo?
His furniture was sold by auction.	Se vendiéron sus muebles en venduta.
She deserves to be happy.	Merece ser feliz.
That affair almost ruined him.	Ese negocio casi le arruinó.
You ought to pay them a visit.	Debe V. hacerles una visita.
He says so, but he does not think it.	Lo dice, pero no lo cree.
I saw him go by just now.	Le ví pasar hace poco.
He spoke to you, and not to him.	Le habló á V., y no á él.
Do you not fear to displease him?	No tiene V. miedo de disgustarle?
You are not yet of an age to make observations.	V. no está todavía en edad de hacer observaciones.
I hope his visits to his uncle are not selfish.	Espero que sus visitas en casa de su tio no son interesadas.
I will thank you for a sheet of paper	Hágame el favor de un pliego de papel.
That play delighted the audience.	Esa comedia agradó mucho al auditorio.
I will give it to you immediately.	Yo se lo daré á V. al instante.
Will you have done soon?	Acabará V. pronto?
Why do you not always get up early?	Porqué no se levanta V siempre temprano?
I shall say nothing but what is true.	No diré mas que la verdad
He writes very sensibly.	Escribe con mucho tino

I will leave you this very day.	Le dejo á V. hoy mismo
I can no longer conceal my resentment from you.	No puedo mas esconderle á V. mi resentimiento.
He seldom goes alone to the country.	Rara vez va solo al campo.
How long is it since you returned from France?	Cuanto hace que V. volvió de Fráncia?
I! see him again! No, never!	¡Yo! volver á verle! Nunca!
We have been hunting for it these two hours.	Hace dos horas que lo estamos buscando.
I will not stay; I shall be back presently.	No me quedaré; vuelvo pronto.
How can we go out without being seen?	Como podemos salir sin que nos vean?
He rewarded those of his servants who had served him faithfully.	Recompensó á los criados que le habian servido con fidelidad.
We met him this evening in the public walks.	Le encontrámos esta tarde en el paseo público.
He had promised it to me, and he gave it to me.	Me lo habia prometido, y me lo dió.
That young man neglects study, therefore he will never be fit for anything.	Ese jóven descuida el estudio; de consiguiente nunca servirá para nada.
I prefer a country-house to the finest palace.	Prefiero una casa de campo al mas bello palacio.
will take her to Paris the first time I go there	La llevaré á Paris la primera vez que vaya.
That cannot be expressed in a few words	Eso no se puede esplicar en pocas palabras.

They spend their fortune.	Gastan su fortuna
This woman's conduct appears extraordinary.	La conducta de esta mujer parece estraordinaria.
She has been lame from her birth.	Está coja desde que nació.
How did he behave during my absence?	Como se condujo durante mi ausencia?
She was living, not long ago.	Vivia hace poco.
This ridiculous story made everybody laugh.	Este cuento ridículo hizo reir á todo el mundo.
Is there anybody dissatisfied in this house?	Hay alguno de esta casa que no está satisfecho?
I have written to the best friend I have.	He escrito al mejor amigo que tengo.
I have always sacrificed my interest to yours.	Siempre he sacrificado mi interes al de V.
She had promised to take me into the country this evening.	Habia prometido llevarme al campo esta tarde.
We all of us go to the theatre to-night.	Vamos todos á la comedia esta noche.
Comedy was brought to perfection by Moliere.	La comedia fué perfeccionada por Moliere.
The nightingale loves to sing when all other birds are silent.	El ruiseñor gusta cantar cuando todos los demas pájaros estan callados.
Everybody admires the uncommon and beautiful flowers of your garden.	Todos se quedan admirados de las flores raras y hermosas de su jardin de V.
Your fortune is at stake.	V. corre el riesgo de perder su fortuna.
He is deep in debt.	Debe mucho.

They have concerts every night.	Tienen conciertos todas las noches.
I will neither write to you nor to them.	No le escribiré á V. ni á ellos.
They shall not fight in my presence.	No lucharan en mi presencia.
I returned it to him yesterday.	Se lo devolví ayer.
How many servants have you?	Cuantos criados tiene V.?
We have four.	Tenemos cuatro.
How good you are to have remembered me!	¡Que bueno es V. en haberse acordado de mí!
I have come to fulfil my promise.	Vengo para cumplir mi palabra.
There is nothing solid in that book.	No hay nada sólido en ese libro.
This piano is out of tune.	Este piano está desafinado.
We expect them every day.	Les esperamos á cada instante.
It is true there is some coolness between them.	Es verdad que hay cierta frialdad entre ellos.
I do not believe he has been as far as that	No creo que fué tan léjos
You came too soon.	V. vino demasiado temprano.
Answer me by return of post.	Contésteme á vuelta de correo.
Was he not then in Europe?	No estaba entónces en Europa?
As for me, I get up very early to write.	Yo me levanto muy temprano, para escribir.
She is unfit for anything.	No sirve para nada.

He embarked yesterday evening at ten o'clock.	Se embarcó ayer á las diez de la noche.
These spots will disappear by degrees.	Estas manchas desapareceran poco á poco.
I do not like them so much as you do.	No me gustan á mí como á V.
How could I grant so unreasonable a request?	Como podia yo condescender á tan irracionable demanda?
If your father and mother think so, they are mistaken.	Si lo creen sus padres de V., estan equivocados.
Excuse the trouble I give you.	Perdone V. la molestia que le doy.
They say that beer is a wholesome drink.	Dicen que la cerveza es una bebida muy sana.
Such long visits become troublesome.	Visitas tan largas son molestas.
She is careless in everything.	Se descuida de todo.
I hate whimsical people.	No me gustan los caprichosos.
She is too obstinate to confess it.	Es demasiado obstinada para confesarlo.
He went out very much displeased.	Salió muy disgustado.
Your hands are as cold as ice.	V. tiene las manos frias como la nieve.
He does everything with the greatest care.	Hace todo con el mayor cuidado.
She is never discouraged.	Nunca está desanimada.
He is an honest man, you can trust him.	Es hombre honrado, puede V. fiarle.

I have had a dreadful head-ache these two days.	Hace dos dias que tengo un dólor de cabeza terrible.
This is a fine picture, put a frame to it.	Es pintura hermosa; mándele V. poner un cuadro.
Do you not know what you are accused of?	No sabe V. de que le acusan?
I shall go home as soon as I have done.	Iré á casa cuando haya acabado.
She did not surely tell you so.	Seguramente no le dijo á V. eso.
See that child; with what pleasure he plays!	Mire ese niño; ¡con que gusto juega!
He gives himself a great deal of trouble.	Se molesta mucho.
He loves his children, and he is loved by them.	Ama á sus niños, y sus niños le aman.
Translate this passage, word for word.	Traduzca este pasage literalmente.
It is the least you can do.	Es lo ménos que V. puede hacer.
This city is large and populous.	Esta villa es grande y muy poblada.
Are you fond of reading?	Le gusta á V. la lectura?
I shall go nowhere to-day.	Hoy no voy ninguna parte.
He never fails to do it every day.	Nunca deja de hacerlo todos los dias.
I acknowledge all that; let us speak no more of it.	Lo reconozco todo; no hablemos mas de eso.
I will judge of it when I am better informed.	Formaré un juício cuando tenga mejores datos.

Do not be inconsistent.	No sea V. inconsecuente
But few people will imitate you in that.	Poca gente le imitaran a V. en eso.
The cottage is built on the hill.	La casita está construida sobre el collado.
sent her all the strawberries I had gathered.	Le mandé todas las fresas que habia cojido.
I was surprised to find the drawer wide open.	Me sorprendió encontrar el cajon abierto.
That argument is not conclusive.	Ese argumento no es concluyente.
He possesses very extensive knowledge.	Posee conocimientos muy vastos.
Nothing could have happened more seasonably.	No podria haber sucedido nada mas oportuno.
It is very evident that such was his project.	Es claro que tal fué su proyecto.
I know him by his voice.	Le conozco por su voz.
Come back as soon as you can.	Vuelva V. lo mas pronto posible.
You have not improved his mind.	V. no ha mejorado su entendimiento.
That drawing is from nature.	Ese dibujo es tomado de la naturaleza.
Why are so many persons employed in that work?	Porqué se emplean tantas personas en esa obra?
I experienced that loss when I least thought of it.	Esperimenté esa pérdida, cuando ménos lo pensaba.
It wounds me to the soul.	Me hiere hasta el alma.
How can you be insensible to all my remonstrances?	Como puede V. ser insensible á todas mis amonestaciones?

Our garden is a hundred feet long.	Nuestro jardin tiene cien. pies de largo.
That is no answer.	Eso no es contestar.
We don't believe they will come to-day.	No creemos que vengan hoy.
He certainly did not mean to affront her.	Es cierto que no la quiso ofender.
Those amiable children are very attentive to their mother's instructions.	Esos niños amables son muy atentos á las instrucciones de su madre.
Do you intend to spend the winter at Boston?	Piensa V. pasar el invierno en Boston?
In the French language, rhyme is used in all poetry.	En la lengua francesa, la rhyma se usa en toda clase de poesia.
They are glad not to have accepted your offer.	Se alegran de no haber aceptado su oferta.
I will go and visit you to-morrow.	Iré visitarle á V. mañana
His morals are exemplary.	Su moral es ejemplar.
I see nothing that can be censured in your conduct.	No veo nada que se puede censurar en su conducta.
Friendship authorises useful advice.	La amistad da lugar á útiles consejos.
Do not imagine you have convinced me.	No se imagine V. que me ha convencido.
I am delighted that everything has been amicably settled.	Me alegro que todo se haya arreglado amigablemente.
This great man will ever be the glory of his country.	Este hombre grande será siempre la gloria de su patria.

Let us sit down under the shade of this tree.	Sentémonos á la sombra de este árbol.
This is a man-of-war, or I am much mistaken.	Es buque de guerra, ó me equivoco mucho.
This is what I think, and nobody shall ever persuade me to the contrary.	Es lo que yo creo, y nadie puede convencerme de lo contrario.
I have a mind to ask him something.	Tengo gana de preguntarle alguna cosa.
I have warned them more than once of the danger they are in.	Les he advertido mas de una vez de su peligro.
Since they have deceived you, do not trust them any more.	Pues que le han engañado, no les fie V. mas.
I was too busy to see you.	Estaba demasiado ocupado para verle á V.
He could not resist the entreaties of his son.	No pudo resistir las súplicas de su hijo.
There is a grace in everything she does.	Hay gracia en todo lo que hace.
He will translate that work.	Traducira esa obra.
Did you see any fish in the market?	Vió V. pescado en la plaza?
They are sorry not to have come.	Sienten no haber venido.
Attend to your business.	Atienda V. á sus negocios
That physician attends him.	Ese médico le visita.
That young lady is attended by several masters.	Esa Señorita toma lecciones de varios maestros.

We have lost all hope, all comfort.	Hemos perdido toda esperanza, todo consuelo.
Let us walk round the garden.	Démos una vuelta en el jardin.
Take care to inform me whether you have received my letter.	No deje V. de avisarme si V. recibe mi carta.
Remember me kindly to her.	Dígale muchas cosas de mi parte.
I anticipated the pleasure of this visit.	Anticipé el gusto de esta visita.
What concerns him is, that he is thought guilty.	Lo que le da cuidado es, que le creen culpable.
I have not seen her ever since we fell out.	No la he visto desde que reñimos.
You thought her handsome, but she is not.	V. la creia bonita, pero no lo es.
Perhaps I was not sufficiently prudent.	Acaso no era bastante prudente.
The hatred of that man will be less dangerous than you think.	El odio de aquel hombre será ménos peligroso de lo que V. piensa.
She listened to his proposal with an air of unqualified astonishment.	Escuchó su proposicion con un ayre de asombro sin igual.
We rarely get rid of our old prejudices.	Rara vez nos zafamos de nuestros perjuicios.
I hope I shall find several letters on my arrival at B...	Espero encontrar algunas cartas al llegar á B...
You make use too often of that term.	V. se sirve demasiado amenudo de ese término.

I never go out but I take cold.	Nunca salgo sin cojer frio.
He was killed by a cannon ball.	Murió de un cañonazo.
I take great care never to remain idle.	Tengo buen cuidado de nunca estar ocioso.
Let us wait for his return.	Esperémos que vuelva.
Do you bring good news?	Trae V. buenas noticias?
A spark may cause a great conflagration.	Una centella puede causar un gran incendio.
This beautiful moonlight invites me to take a walk.	Esta hermosa luna me convida al paséo.
We have had a great eclipse of the sun this year.	Hemos tenido una gran eclipse de sol este año.
I see it in a very different light.	Lo veo de bien diferente modo.
She begins to grow old.	Comienza á envejecer.
The ass is a patient and laborious animal.	El burro es animal muy paciente y laborioso.
We attended at his funeral.	Hemos asistido á su entierro.
I will give you all the money I have.	Le daré todo el dinero que tengo.
We ought to sacrifice pleasure to duty.	Debemos sacrificar el placer al deber.
The reason why he is arrested is known.	La razon porqué está arrestado es conocida.
What I cannot bear is insolence and treachery.	Lo que no puedo aguantar: son la insolencia y la traicion.
He is very anxious to please.	Hace todo lo posible para agradar.

She dresses with taste.	Se viste con gusto.
He sold his house last week.	Vendió su casa la semana pasada.
You have given me a great deal of trouble.	V. me ha dado mucha molestia.
Do you prefer your flowers to mine?	Prefiere V. sus flores á las mias?
Pay attention to what I say.	Atiende á lo que te digo
I do all I can, don't I?	Hago lo que puedo, ¿no es verdad?
My drawing-master is not yet come.	No vino todavia el maestro de dibujo.
There are things about which you do not think	Hay cosas en que V. no piensa.
What a noise they make!	¡Que ruido estan haciendo!
He thinks he can do that alone.	Cree poder hacerlo solo.
How shall I prevent that?	Como puedo yo remediarlo?
Are you the ladies whom my mother expected?	Son ustedes las Señoras que esperaba mi madre?
May you not be disappointed in your hopes!	¡Que sus esperanzas se realizen!
As for me, I shall not be his dupe.	Lo que es á mí, no me engañará.
This greyhound exceeds the fox in swiftness.	Este galgo escede en velocidad á la zorra.
They enjoy a pure and wholesome air in France.	En Francia se goza de un ayre puro y sano.
How old would you suppose him to be?	Que edad le supondria V.?

Goats like to graze on sloping hills.	Las cabras gustan pacer en collados de poca pendiente.
This action does you great honour.	Esta accion le honra á V. mucho.
It is easy for you to say so.	Es muy fácil que V. lo diga.
They tell us freely of our faults.	Nos reprenden nuestras faltas libremente.
It is a long time since you came to see us.	Hace mucho tiempo que V. no vino á vernos.
I do not see what great honour there is in doing such a thing.	No veo que gran honor hay en hacer cosa semejante.
I have it from good authority.	Lo sé de buena autoridad.
I am well aware of the danger of that enterprise.	Bien conozco el peligro de esa empresa.
Were there many young people?	Habia muchos jóvenes?
This is my stick, which is yours?	Este baston es mio, ¿cual es él de V.?
Shall I repeat his words?	Quiere V. que repita sus palabras?
The tempest dispersed all the vessels.	La tempestad esparció todos los barcos.
The boy is backward in his learning.	El muchacho está muy atrasado en su educacion.
What books are you speaking of?	De que libros habla V.?
Is this your horse?	Es el caballo de V.?
Yes, it is.	Sí Señor.
What have they done?	Que han hecho?

What are you doing, daughter?	Que háces, hija?
I am reading, father.	Estoy leyendo, papá.
Whatever happens, let me know it.	Sea lo que fuera, dímelo
I am very angry with them.	Estoy muy enfadado con ellos.
To-morrow I shall be at home at five o'clock.	Mañana estaré en casa á las cinco.
I did myself the honour to call on you,	Tuve el honor de pasar á su casa.
This horse is as quiet as a lamb.	Este caballo parece un cordero.
These are empty arguments that will persuade no one.	Estos son argumentos vacios que á nadie convéncen.
The church is built on the declivity of a hill.	La iglesia está construida en la pendiente de una colina.
Six of us are going into the country, will you join us?	Vámos seis de nosotros al campo, ¿quiere V. acompañarnos?
A table two feet long and two inches thick.	Una mesa de dos pies de largo, y dos pulgadas de grueso.
I request you to make my compliments to him when you see him.	Hágame V. el favor de darle memorias, cuando V. le vea.
He knew how to excite the emulation of his pupils.	Sabia escitar la emulacion de sus discípulos.
Somebody knocks at the door, see who it is	Tocan á la puerta; vaya á ver quien es.
He tries to vex you.	Trata de vejarle á V.

May and September are the two finest months of the year in France.	En Francia, los meses de Mayo y Setiembre son los mas bellos del año.
You do not go the right way about it.	V. no va bien.
We cannot love those who are wicked.	No podemos querer á los necios.
Do you think she did right?	Cree V. que hizo bien?
I defy anyone to convince me of having done it.	Desafio á cualquiera que me convenza de haberlo hecho.
How have I deserved this treatment from you?	Como he merecido el tratamiento que V. me da?
Will your father be at home this evening?	Su padre estará en casa esta noche?
I have returned his visit.	He pagado su visita.
If you sell your horses, you will lose by them	V. perderá, si vende sus caballos.
Take down that picture.	Quite V. ese cuadro.
Where would your brother have slept?	En donde hubiera dormido su hermano?
What is it to me whether you do it or no?	Que mas me da á mí, si lo haces ó no?
I am much obliged to you for your attention.	Muchas grácias por su atencion.
Why wish to deprive me of that innocent pleasure?	Porqué querer quitarme ese placer inocente?
It is the same man I saw yesterday at church.	Es el mismo hombre que ví ayer en la iglesia.
You certainly have many advantages over him.	Por supuesto que V. tiene mas ventajas que él.

thought your brother was to be of the party.	Creí que su hermano iba á ser de la partida.
Where would your sisters have remained?	En donde se habrían quedado sus hermanas?
I cannot tell what sort of weather it will be to-morrow.	No sé que tiempo tendrémos mañana.
Perhaps we shall have a happier fate.	Acaso tendrémos una suerte mas dichosa.
That passage is dangerous on account of the rocks.	Ese pasage es muy peligroso, por causa de las peñas.
Do not carry matters further.	No lleve V. mas adelante ese asunto.
Will you have the cruelty to abandon me?	Tendrá V. la crueldad de abandonarme?
I have seen him in the garden.	Le he visto en la huerta.
This is the fifth or sixth time I have told you of it.	Es la quinta ó la sesta vez que te lo he dicho.
I am much obliged to you for the pains you have taken.	Le estoy muy agradecido por la moléstia que V se ha tomado.
Do not stir from your place.	No se menée V. de su sítio.
Since I must choose one of those two rooms, I like this better than the other.	Pues tengo que escojer uno de esos dos cuartos, me gusta mas este que el otro.
Does your friend improve in the French language?	Su amigo adelanta mucho en la lengua francesa?
There is no harm in that.	No hay daño en eso.

Tell her to ask for your sister's book.	Dígale que pida el libro de su hermana.
He is an acquaintance of mine.	Es conocido mio.
This savours of affectation.	Esto parece afectacion.
They have undergone great misfortunes.	Han padecido muchas desgracias.
Would you blame him if he should own it?	Le culparia V., si lo confesara.
She does herself a great deal of harm.	Se daña mucho.
I beg you would make my apology to him.	Suplico á V. que me escuse con él.
His condition is not worth envying.	No se debe envidiarle su condicion.
Remember to come to-morrow at the same hour.	Acuérdate de venir mañana á la misma hora.
Do not the most powerful empires fall?	No caen los imperios los mas poderosos?
She learns French and Italian.	Estudia el Frances y el Italiano.
I thank you for the honour you do me.	Estimo mucho el honor que V. me hace.
It is the easiest thing in the world.	Es la cosa mas fácil del mundo.
As soon as dinner was over, she disappeared.	Al acabarse la comida, desapareció.
If you wish to see fine pictures, he has some.	Si V. quiere ver pinturas hermosas, él las tiene.
You do not eat anything: what ails you?	V. no come nada: ¿que tiene?
Put me in mind of that.	Acuérdeme de eso.

She has been brought up with the utmost care.	Ha sido criada con mucho cuidado.
What is the matter with you?	Que tiene V.?
I do not know what to do with them.	No sé que hacer con ellos.
We must use ourselves to work.	Debemos acostumbrarnos al trabajo.
Have a little more prudence.	Tenga V. un poco mas prudencia.
Even then he did it with a bad grace.	Aun entónces lo hizo de mala gana.
Do not be impatient, I will be back presently.	Tenga V. paciencia, vuelvo luego.
What shall I do? I, who have not a friend in the world!	Que haré? yo, que no tengo siquiera un amigo en el mundo!
I shall spend the evening with you at Mrs. D...'s.	Pasaré la noche con V. en casa de la Señora D...
I was very sorry to hear a calamity had befallen him.	Sentí mucho oir que le habia sucedido una desgracia.
They are assisted by the ablest masters.	Tienen la ayuda de los mejores maestros.
We do not neglect anything to please you.	No omitimos nada que pueda gustarle á V.
What I said to you this evening, is true.	Lo que le he dicho esta noche, es verdad.
He takes the lead in conversation.	Se toma la mayor parte en la conversacion.
As soon as we were acquainted with the danger he was in, we ran to his assistance.	Al instante que supímos el peligro en que se encontraba, fuímos á su socorro.

Go to that spring to drink: the water is delightful.	Vaya beber á esa fuente; el agua es deliciosa.
Shall we subject ourselves to his caprice?	Debemos sujetarnos á sus caprichos?
Have you not perceived your mistake.	No ha visto V. su equivocacion?
If you chance to hear from him, let me know.	Si acaso V. recibe carta de él, mándemelo V. á decir.
We have been astonished to hear of her marriage.	Nos sorprendímos al oir su matrimonio.
I had done before he arrived.	Habia acabado ántes que él llegara.
He hinders me from doing it.	No me deja hacerlo.
She has married a man without education.	Se casó con un hombre sin educacion.
She has a melancholy and thoughtful look.	Tiene el ayre melancólico y pensativo.
They call him an honest man; I call him a rogue.	Pasa por hombre honrado; yo le llamo pillo.
You speak very quick; a great deal too quick.	V. habla muy de prisa, demasiado á prisa.
That is not a question to be asked.	Es pregunta que no se debe hacer.
He is more sincere than he should be.	Es mas sincero de lo que debe ser.
He is a friend in whom I can put my confidence.	Es amigo en quien puedo fiarme.
I am fond of cherries, but I see none here.	Me gustan mucho las guindas, pero no veo aquí.
I know that to a certainty.	Lo sé hasta la evidencia.

He buys books to adorn his room, for he never reads.	Compra libros para adornar su cuarto, pues nunca lée.
How long have you been at variance?	Cuanto hace que estan Vs. enemistados?
How many young ladies did you see at the ball?	Cuantas Señoritas vio V. al baile?
I hope his industry will lead to fortune.	Espero que su industria le conducirá á la fortuna.
You and he are inclined to believe the contrary.	V. y él estan dispuestos á creer lo contrario.
This day se'nnight I will call on you.	Le pasaré á ver de hoy en ocho dias.
Let them be ready to set out at four.	Que esten listos para marchar á las cuatro.
This house has a fine prospect.	Esta casa tiene buena vista.
If we let them alone, they will spoil everything.	Si los dejamos, lo echaran á perder todo.
He was only thirteen years old.	No tenia mas que trece años.
Why should you not work, since I work myself?	Porqué no trabajaria V.? pues trabajo yo.
That is not worth mentioning.	No merece mencionarse.
How do you happen to be here at this time of night?	Como sucede que V está aquí á esta hora de la noche?
Do not over-heat yourselves with running.	No se sofoquen Vs con tanto correr.
We will do it without faults.	Lo harémos sin errores.
They imposed upon you.	Le engañaron á V

All is lost! our conversation was overheard.	¡Todo está perdido nuestra conversacion ha sido oida.
Have you already studied geography and history?	Has estudiado ya la geografia y la historia?
The bodily constitution has a great effect on the mind.	La constitucion del cuerpo influye mucho en el entendimiento.
You would go too much out of your way if you took that road.	V. se alejaria demasiado de su camino, si fuera por ahí.
The publication of that history added nothing to his reputation.	La publicacion de esa historia no añadió nada á su reputacion.
I think myself honoured by your acquaintance.	Me honro con su conocimiento.
She is on the point of being angry.	Está á punto de enfadarse.
If you have no other fear, be easy.	Si no teme V. otra cosa, puede tranquilizarse.
After I had been waiting for him two hours, he came.	Vino, despues que le habia esperado dos horas.
Bring me the fork which is on the table.	Tráeme el tenedor que está encima de la mesa.
I shall probably see him to-morrow.	Puede ser que le vea mañana.
The pit began immediately to cry: hats off!	La gente del patio comenzáron á gritar: ¡fuera sombreros!
I was deprived of the pleasure of seeing him.	Me priváron del placer de verle.
Let us apply ourselves to mathematics.	Estudiémos las matemáticas.

There is no room for hesitation; one must submit to that.	No hay lugar a duda; es necesario someterse á ello.
When you come, you will find me ready.	Cuando V. venga, me hallará V. listo.
I can speak when I am writing.	Puedo hablar cuando estoy escribiendo.
I do it, and so ought you.	Yo lo hago, debe V. hacerlo tambien.
He has been very near dying.	Le faltó poco para morir.
I had soon exhausted my resources.	Todos los recursos se me habian acabado.
Can you give me a night's lodging?	Puede V. alojarme esta noche?
He seems to have done it to contradict you.	Parece que lo hizo para contradecirle.
I will send for him, and he shall be punished.	Yo le mandaré buscar, y será castigado.
I am sorry that my work displeases you, but I did my best.	Siento que mi trabajo no le gustó, pero he hecho lo mejor que pude.
These walks are well kept, I like to see their regularity.	Estas calles estan bien conservadas; me gusta su regularidad.
I prefer red to black, and she likes green better than blue.	Yo prefiero el encarnado al negro; á ella le gusta mas el verde que el azul.
He seems prudent; he is however by no means so.	Parece prudente; pero no lo es de ningun modo.
You will not get much by it	V. no ha de ganar mucho en eso.

He has, it is said, neither friends nor foes.	Se dice que no tiene amigos ni enemigos.
A vulgar man is captious and jealous, eager and impetuous about trifles.	Un hombre vulgar es capcioso y celoso, anxioso é impetuoso, en las cosas mas insignificantes.
Caprice may have charms for some, and to them I leave it.	Los caprichos tienen sus encantos para algunos, y para los tales los dejo.
The duty of a fabulist is to instruct while he amuses.	El deber de un novelista es instruir deleitando.
We could not have walked faster.	No podríamos haber an dado mas pronto.
The whole question amounted to this.	Toda la cuestion se reducia á esto
He attacked the enemy in their very camp.	Atacó al enemigo en sus mismas trincheras.
You cannot think what trouble I had to make him come.	No puede V. imaginarse la pena que tenia en hacerle venir.
When he has been punished, he will pay more attention.	Despues que le hayan castigado, pondrá mas atencion.
We shall do it in spite of everybody.	Lo harémos, á pesar del mundo entero.
Were I in your place, I would do it.	Yo lo haria, si estuviera en su lugar.
I lost my watch last week, but a friend of yours found it.	Perdí mi relox la semana pasada, pero un amigo de V. lo encontró.
I feel all the unpleasantness of your situation.	Siento todo lo desagradable de su situacion
Come, to the point	Vámos, al punto.

You make promise upon promise, but there is no dependence upon you.	V. ha hecho pron.esa sobre promesa, pero no se puede depender de V.
He has been at college these four years.	Hace cuatro años que está en el colejio.
If the undertaking is considerable, I will go halves with you.	Si la empresa lo merece, voy á mitad con V.
Yesterday fortnight I went out for the first time.	Ayer hace quince dias que salí por la primera vez.
It is the utmost, if you get half of what he owes you.	Si V. coja la mitad de lo que le debe, es lo mas.
I was told he lives contentedly.	Me han dicho que vive contento.
He was presented to the king.	Fué presentado al rey.
I have invited some friends, some very good friends.	He convidado algunos amigos, algunos buenos amigos.
There is nothing to criticise.	No hay nada que criticar.
He has conquered several provinces.	Ha conquistado varias provincias.
Does your mother go out so soon?	Sale su madre de V. tan temprano?
I have found it: here it is.	Lo he encontrado: aquí está.
Shall I call upon you on Friday or Saturday?	Quiere V. que pase á su casa Viérnes ó Sábado.
He is the most diligent of the whole school.	Es el mas diligente de toda la escuela.
Lucy is fifteen years old.	Lucia tiene quince años.

That is your advice, but it is not ours.	Eso es su consejo, pero no el nuestro.
Though I have foreseen that accident, I could not avoid it.	Aunque he previsto ese accidente, no lo podio evitar.
I softened my father by my submission.	He ablandado á mi padre por medio de mi sumision.
Let us see if everything is right.	A ver si todo va bien,
The moment he comes, send me word.	Al instante que venga, mándemelo á decir.
Sit down by me.	Siéntese V. á mi lado.
Wit, beauty, youth, riches: she possesses everything.	Talento, hermosura, juventud, riquezas: todo lo posée.
I have deserved this affront, said Maria, bursting into tears.	He merecido este insulto, dijo María, bañados los ojos en lágrimas.
A woman who has not maintained a proper respect for herself, is not to expect it from others.	Mujer que no se ha respetado á si misma, no lo puede esperar de otros.
The heat is very oppressive.	El calor está muy sofocante.
I enjoy the most perfect health.	Gozo de una salud inmejorable.
His mother scolded him often.	Su madre le regañaba muy amenudo.
Let them forsee what may happen.	Que prevean lo que puede suceder.
Wooden houses are dangerous.	Las casas de madera son peligrosas

We should not be received if we came too late.	No nos recibirian si llegásemos demasiado tarde.
No one behaves better than he does.	Nadie se conduce mejor que él.
We have seen his sisters; they are very beautiful.	Hemos visto á sus hermanas; son muy lindas.
I like the country; I am going there for three months.	Me gusta el campo; voy á pasar tres meses en él.
There are two women who ask to speak with you.	Hay dos mujeres que quieren hablar con V.
He read the novel, then he lent it to me.	Leyó la novela, y despues me la prestó.
I was at his house this day se'nnight.	Estaba en su casa hace hoy ocho dias.
You press the matter home upon me.	V. me apura demasiado.
He was not killed; he died a natural death.	No fué asesinado; murió de muerte natural.
Truth and beauty are the objects of the arts.	La verdad y la hermosura son los objetos de las artes.
Once more, Sir, leave off your importunities.	Una vez mas, Señor, deje V. de importunar.
She boasts of her father being a nobleman, and I believe he is a plebeian.	Se vanagloria que su padre es noble, y á mi parecer es plebeyo.
She wrote me word that her father-in-law was at the point of death.	Me escribió que su suegro estaba á punto de morir.
I will foretell what will happen.	Yo le diré lo que sucederá.
Nothing frightens him.	Nada le atemoriza.

You impair your health; he takes care of his.	V. daña su salud, él cuida la suya.
I should like to read Moliere's works.	Me gustaria leer las obras de Moliere.
The dog which followed you is mine.	El perro que siguió á V es mio.
We have displeased your friend.	Hemos ofendido á su amigo.
If you are satisfied, I am not.	Si V está satisfecho, yo no lo estoy.
I must write a letter before dinner.	Me es menester escribir una carta, ántes de comer.
I will soon answer your letter.	Pronto contestaré su carta de V.
The greater was his success, the more modest he was.	Tanto mayor era su fortuna, tanto mas modesto era él
He used injurious language to him.	Usó con él un lenguage insultante.
He suppressed several interesting circumstances.	Suprimió muchas circunstancias interesantes.
I ask you a favour and you refuse it me, although you owe to me everything you have.	Te pido un favor y me lo rehusas, aunque me debes todo lo que tienes.
The less I dance, the less I shall fatigue myself.	Tanto ménos bailo, ménos me cansaré.
How much does that man earn a week?	Cuanto gana ese hombre por semana?
Here is your nosegay, Miss Lucy	Aquí está su boquet, Señorita Lucia.
Buy that for me at any price.	Cómpreme eso á cualquier precio

Lend me that book, if you can do without it.	Préstame ese libro si no lo necesitas.
It is late in the night; we can't stay any longer.	Ya es tarde; no podemos quedarnos mas.
There is great pleasure in silencing great talkers.	Es un placer imponer silencio á los grandes habladores.
I shall probably see him to-morrow.	Acaso le veré mañana.
Why do you descend to useless particulars?	Porqué desciende V. á minuciosidades inútiles?
Did you ever hear such a discourse?	Ha oido V. jamas un discurso semejante?
Has that officer any merit?	Tiene algun mérito ese oficial?
To-morrow will be a holiday.	Mañana será dia de fiesta.
You hurt nobody but yourself.	V. no daña á nadie sino á si mismo.
That house projects too much in the street.	Esta casa sobresale demasiado á la calle.
That imprudent step is sufficient to ruin you.	Ese paso imprudente basta para arruinarle á V.
He can do a great deal in the business in question.	Puede hacer mucho en ese negocio.
He is never happy but when he is out of the house.	No está contento, sino estando fuera de casa.
You always speak of me when I am out of the house.	V. habla siempre de mi cuando estoy fuera de casa.
It is almost three weeks since I saw her last.	Hace casi tres semanas que no la ví.

Have they spoken of it?	Han hablado de eso?
Whatever happens, I will come to your house.	De todos modos iré á su casa de V.
Bestow some charity upon him; as for me, I cannot afford it.	Hágale V. alguna caridad lo que es por mí, no me es posible.
Take neither this flower nor that.	No tomes esta flor, ni esa tampoco.
He loves reading as much as you love play.	Le gusta leer, como á tí te gusta jugar.
Must he be insolent because he is rich?	Ha de ser insolente porque es rico?
It is for that reason I do not grant his request.	Esta es la razon porque no accedo á su súplica
As we shall not breakfast till ten o'clock, we have half-an-hour to spare.	Como no almorzamos hasta las diez, tenemos todavia media hora.
What have you done since you have been here?	Que ha hecho V. desde que está aquí?
I told you that I had been waiting for him these three days.	Ya le he dicho que le esperaba hace tres dias.
Such conduct is blameable.	Conducta semejante es culpable.
That is right; no, that is wrong.	Eso es; no, no es eso.
Everybody speaks well of him.	Todos hablan bien de él
My friends pity me, but do not relieve me.	Mis amigos me compadecen, pero no me socorren.
I could produce a thousand examples of it.	Produciria mil ejemplares de eso

I will wait upon you without fail.	Pasaré á su casa de V. sin falta ninguna.
Why do you laugh at us?	Porqué se rie V. de nosotros?
That is mine, give it me back again.	Eso es mio, devuélvamelo otra vez.
There were so many people that one could not stir.	Habia tanta gente, que no se podia uno mover.
What rejoices me is to hear you are in good health.	Lo que me gusta es saber que V. goza de buena salud.
That does not become you, any more than me.	Eso no le viene bien á V., mas que á mí.
Put your books into their places again.	Pon tus libros en su lugar.
We are not new acquaintances.	No hace poco que nos conocemos.
I know what has happened.	Sé lo que ha sucedido.
Shall I have the honour of dining with you to-morrow?	Tendré el honor de comer con V, mañana?
The most you can expect is twenty dollars.	Lo mas que V. puede esperar, son veinte pesos.
He takes an interest in your welfare.	Se interesa en su bienestar.
Call me when it is time.	Llámeme cuando sea tiempo.
His house is quite different from what it was.	Su casa es muy diferente de lo que era.
It does not become you to keep such bad company	No le viene bien tener compañia semejante.
I intend to write to them this day week.	Voy á escribirles, de hoy en ocho dias

Is it you, gentlemen, we must thank?	Son ustedes, Señores, á quienes debémos dar las gracias?
Happy mother! your children will be the comfort of your old age.	¡Madre feliz! vuestros hijos seran el consuelo de vuestra vejez!
That bespeaks a good temper.	Esto revela un buen temperamento.
I will let you my house, on condition that you do the repairs.	Yo le alquilaré mi casa. á condicion que V. haga los reparos.
As long as I have money, you shall not want any.	Miéntras yo tenga dinero. no le faltará á V.
I take it upon myself; be no longer uneasy.	Yo me encargo de eso; descuide V.
Assist him with your advice.	Ayúdele V. con sus consejos.
She pays her music-master a dollar a lesson.	Paga á su maestro de música un peso por leccion.
We have seven minutes to spare.	Tenemos todavia siete minutos.
He has been gone out almost an hour.	Ya hace casi una hora que salió.
Do you know what I think?	Sabes lo que creo?
How long has he been dead?	Cuanto hace que murió?
Will you employ the means I point out to you?	Se servirá V. de los medios que yo le indico?
I assure you that this money is not mine.	Le aseguro á V. que este dinero no es mio.
What general commanded on that day?	Que general mandó ese dia?

I shall never recover from my surprise.	Nunca volveré de mi sorpresa.
Have you done so many at once?	Ha hecho V. tantos á la vez?
Why don't you speak? are you dumb?	Porqué no habla V.? es V. mudo?
How long have you lived in Philadelphia?	Cuanto hace que V. vive en Filadelfia?
That is a dreadful idea, and I cannot think of it without shuddering.	Es una idea terrible; no puedo pensar en eso sin temblar.
Don't you think we have walked long enough?	No crée V. que nos hemos paseado bastante?
I shall exert myself for you to the utmost of my power.	Haré todo lo posible para servirle á V.
I must rise at five tomorrow, or even at half-past four.	Es preciso que me levante mañana á las cinco, ó acaso á las cuatro y media.
How does he spend his time since he is with you?	Como pasa el tiempo desde que está con V.?
For my part, I find myself so well here that I am greatly inclined to remain.	Por mi parte, me encuentro tan bien aquí que tengo gana de quedarme.
He fell from his horse and broke his leg.	Cayó de su caballo y se rompió una pierna.
Your father never refuses you what you ask.	Tu padre no te rehusa nunca lo que le pides.
It is dear living at New York.	Es muy caro vivir en Nueva York.
Although he is gone by, I did not see him.	Aunque pasó cerca, no le ví.

I know not what is the matter with me; I find myself out of humour.	No sé lo que tengo; me siento de mal humor.
He did that at my request.	Hizo eso para complacerme.
He did not interfere in that business.	No se mezcló en ese asunto.
They want many conveniences.	Les faltan muchas conveniencias.
This I regard as an act of simple justice	Lo miro solamente como acto de justicia.
Will you tell me what you know of it?	Quiere V. decirme lo que sabe?
Do you not go to the play this evening?	No va V. al teatro esta noche?
You always leave everything in disorder.	Siempre lo dejas todo en desórden.
I think it rather strange that your brother never writes.	Me parece un poco estraño que nunca escriba su hermano de V.
You did not mind what I wrote you.	V. no hizo caso de lo que le escribí.
Who sent for him?	Quién le mandó á buscar?
Did you ever hear anybody speak ill of those ladies?	Ha oido V. jamas hablar mal de esas Señoras?
I will tell you in few words the whole of the matter.	En pocas palabras le diré á V. todo el negocio.
He stands a chance of being very rich one day.	El está en camino para llegar á ser muy rico.
I request that of you as a favour.	Le pido á V. eso como un favor

DETACHED SENTENCES.

You seem very much dejected, tell me what vexes you.	V. parece muy abatido; dígame V. que le aflije.
I shall have done my work before you begin yours.	Habré acabado mi trabajo ántes que V. empiece el suyo.
He has always been good for nothing.	Nunca ha servido para nada.
I hope we shall spend the time pleasantly.	Espero que pasarémos el tiempo agradablemente
I could not restrain myself any longer.	No podia contenerme mas
I am glad she is gone.	Me alegro de que se haya marchado.
We are to go to France next year.	Tenemos que ir á Francia el año que viene.
I don't hesitate about that.	No me paro en eso.
I am afraid to distress you.	Temo afligir á V.
There is a question I dare not ask.	No me atrevo á preguntarle una cosa.
Miss B..., whom you know, is very ill.	La Señorita B..., que V. conoce, está muy mala.
It is a good thing to be here in such weather.	Estamos bien aquí en tiempo semejante.
Who did that? was it you?	Quien hizo eso? fué V.?
It is one of your tricks.	Es uno de sus chascos.
It has been a very severe winter.	Ha sido el invierno muy severo.
It is still excessively cold.	Todavia hace un frio escesivo.
My dear, you increase your happiness by sharing it.	Querida mia, aumentas tu felicidad participandola.

From his youth he was trained to business.	Desde su juventud estuvo entregado á los negocios.
There is a meanness in everything he does.	Es una bajeza todo cuanto hace.
She looks at us without knowing us.	Nos mira sin conocernos.
If you will accompany me, I will show you where I live.	Si V. quiere acompañarme, le enseñaré en donde vivo
He behaves not as he should.	No se conduce como debia.
He gave him a civil reception.	Le recibió con urbanidad
All that she says is pleasing and interesting.	Todo lo que dice divierte é interesa.
I shall see you this day se'nnight, if I am well.	Lo veré á V. de hoy en quince dias, si estoy bueno.
What you have told us is surprising.	Lo que V. nos ha dicho es maravilloso.
In what manner do you intend to spend your holidays?	De que modo piensa V. pasar las vacaciones?
I have no time to give you a lesson.	No tengo tiempo para darle á V. leccion.
Make him listen to reason, if you can.	Hágale V. escuchar la razon, si V. puede.
Did you receive Miss K.'s note?	Recibió V. al billete de la Señorita K.?
I know something which is not calculated to make you merry.	Sé alguna cosa que no es muy á propósito para ponerle alegre.
What are you speaking of?	De que habla V?

You are not yet able to construe that author.	V. no es capaz de construir ese autor.
That which I fear most is treason.	Lo que mas temo es la traicion.
What I like best is to be alone.	Lo que mas me gusta es estar solo.
I think it is going to snow.	Creo que va á nevar.
His imprudence caused him to be discovered.	Su insolencia le hizo descubrir.
The table upon which you write is broken.	La mesa en que V. escribe esta rota.
Do you speak sincerely?	Habla V. con sinceridad?
Do not stop her, she is in great haste.	No la detenga V., tiene mucha prisa.
I will command her to do it.	Le mandaré hacerlo.
How long have you been in America?	Cuanto hace que V. está en América?
Of whom were you speaking when I came in?	De quien hablaba V. cuando entré?
He walks in the yard from morning till night.	Se pasea en el patio todo el dia.
You must begin that work to-day, or else you cannot finish it in time.	Es preciso que V. empiece ese trabajo hoy, sino le será imposible acabarlo á tiempo.
You do not seem to pay attention to what I say to you.	Parece que V. no hace caso de lo que le digo.
Ought I not to pay them a visit?	No debo hacerles una visita?
He walked round the house, and spoke to everybody he met with.	Se paseó alrededor de la casa, y habló á todos los que encontró.

This style is more ornamented than the subject demands.	Este estilo es mas elevado de lo que el objeto requiere.
All those officious persons must be kept at a distance.	Todas estas personas oficiosas, es menester conservarlas á cierta distáncia.
This is unquestionably the best work that has come from the pen of that author.	Sin duda esta es la mejor obra que salió de la pluma de ese autor.
I was told yesterday that you were ill, and I am truly glad to see you look so well.	Me han dicho ayer que V. estaba malo, y me alegro mucho verle á V tan bueno.
Do you not like strawberries?	No le gustan las fresas?
This day fortnight there will be a ball at the assembly-room.	De hoy en quince dias habrá baile en la sala de la asamblea.
Don't light the candles yet.	No enciende todavía las velas.
That which you say is true, but few people believe it.	Lo que V. dice es la verdad, pero pocos lo créen.
He acquainted nobody in the world with his project.	No dejó conocer á nadie su proyecto.
That which I hate in a young man is laziness.	Lo que mas me disgusta en un jóven, es la pereza.
Are you going to the opera to-night?	Va V. á la ópera esta noche?
mentioned it to no one.	No lo he dicho á nadie

He had no time to answer the letters you wrote to him.	No tuvo tiempo de contestar las cartas que V. le escribió.
We want to go out this morning	Queremos salir esta mañana
I should answer Mrs. H.'s letter, but I have no time.	Contestaria la carta de la Señora H., pero no tengo tiempo.
You will spoil your sight if you read by fire light.	Echará V. á perder su vista, si V. lee á la luz del fuego.
Shall we have plenty of cherries this year?	Tendrémos muchas guindas este año?
Have you bought the new pamphlets?	Ha comprado V. los nuevos folletos?
People forget themselves in prosperity.	Todos se olvidan de sí mismos, en la prosperidad.
He made me drink two glasses of wine.	Me hizo beber dos vasos de vino.
That loss will bear hard upon her.	Sentirá muchisimo esa pérdida.
What are you going to do on the other side of the river?	Que va V. á hacer al otro lado del rio?
What could I do without you?	Que haria yo sin V.?
Put her book in its place again.	Vuelva á poner su libro en su lugar.
Ask them to dine with us to-morrow.	Convídelos á comer con nosotros mañana.
Which of the two will you have?	Cual quiere V. de los dos?
I have lost my hat and gloves.	He perdido el sombrero y los guantes.

I could ruin him, but I had rather expose myself to lose everything.	Le podria arruinar, pero mas quiero esponerme á perderlo todo.
I only ask you to go there.	Solo le pido que vaya allá.
Send me my penknife, when you have done with it.	Mándeme mi cortaplumas, cuando haya acabado con él.
That man has no notion of propriety.	Ese hombre no tiene una idea de decencia.
In losing my mother, I have lost everything.	Perdiendo á mi madre, lo he perdido todo.
We should render ourselves despicable.	Nos haríamos despreciables.
I will share with you.	Yo partiré con V.
He works more than any one of you.	Trabaja mas que cualquiera de vosotros.
We shall no doubt see the gardener.	Sin duda verémos al jardinero.
I know that you might have learnt your lesson.	Sé que podrias haber aprendido tu leccion.
I see him yonder, at work.	Le veo allá, trabajando.
This street is nearly finished; it is large and fine.	Está casi acabada esta calle, es grande y hermosa.
's your sister sick?	Está mala su hermana?
We were caught by a storm.	Nos cojió una tempestad.
He did it to make me uneasy.	Lo hizo para molestarme.
He has been all this while amusing himself with trifles.	Todo el rato lo ha pasado divertido en frioleras.
You have courage enough, but you want prudence.	V. tiene bastante valor, pero le falta prudéncia.

His condition is not worth envying.	No vale la pena de envidiarle su condicion.
A man was hanged for having robbed the mail.	Ahorcáron á un hombre por haber robado el correo.
He has not even a competency.	No tiene ni aun lo necesario.
I will see him this minute.	Le veré al instante.
He is praised when he does right, and reprimanded when he does wrong.	Es alabado cuando obra bien, y reprehendido cuando obra mal.
Do not confide in him.	No se fie V. de él.
It is useless to fall into a passion.	Es inútil enfadarse.
He is a good-natured boy, and does not want abilities.	Es muchacho de buen genio, y no le falta capacidad.
We are not pleased with this bargain.	No estamos contentos de esta compra.
Those who were formerly his friends, are now his enemies.	Los que antiguamente eran sus amigos, son ahora sus enemigos.
Have you ever seen anything so beautiful?	Ha visto V. jamas cosa tan bella?
I was present at that ceremony.	Presencié la ceremonia.
He fell from a tower two hundred feet high.	Cayó de una torre de la altura de dos cientos piés.
They returned him their most humble thanks	Le han dado las mas cordiales gracias.
Will you lend me some of your books?	Quiere V. prestarme algunos de sus libros?

Give me leave to introduce you to my sister-in-law's uncle and aunt.	Permítame V. introducirle al tio y á la tia de mi cuñada.
It is with painters as with poets, they are at liberty to employ fiction.	Los pintores como los poetas, tienen la libertad de la ficcion.
I protest there is something in that theme that pleases me.	Le aseguro á V. que hay algo en ese tema que me gusta.
To speak ingenuously, that is a point entirely undetermined at present.	Para hablar con franqueza, es punto que no se ha determinado todavía.
You may set off if you please.	Puede V. marcharse si quiere.
His hand is cold and trembling.	Su mano está temblando de frio.
My happiness depends on yours.	Mi felicidad depende de la de V.
Would you have me borrow of him, to whom I refused to lend?	Quiere V. que pida prestado á aquel, á quien no he querido prestar.
I read Horace and Virgil, because they are the best Latin poets.	Leo á Horacio y Virgilio, porque son los mejores poetas Latinos.
I will hinder him from hurting you.	No le dejaré dañar á V.
We have been taking the air on horseback.	Hemos tomado el ayre á caballo.
Would you cross a river six feet deep?	Pasaria V. un rio de seis piés de profundidad?
I cannot but take a great interest in everything that concerns you.	No puedo ménos de interesarme en todo lo que le toca á V.

My brother will not set off without taking leave of all his friends.	Mi hermano no se marchará sin despedirse de todos sus amigos.
Put each of these papers into its place again.	Vuelva á poner estos papeles cada uno en su lugar.
Her chin is exceedingly long, and her brother's mouth is uncommonly wide.	Tiene la barba muy larga, y la boca de su hermano es muy ancha.
I am going to call on your relations, and give them an account of your conduct.	Voy á pasar en casa de tus padres, y darles cuenta de tu conducta.
Let us go faster, for it is going to rain.	Andémos mas pronto, pues va á llover.
I should have written yesterday to my sister.	Debia haber escrito á mi hermana ayer.
It is a long time since we have seen him.	Hace mucho tiempo que no le hemos visto.
He has written his exercise, but he did not read the rules.	Ha escrito su tema, pero no leyó las reglas.
Why did she not come and tell me so herself?	Porqué no vino á decirmelo ella misma?
If he has lost his money, he must not lay the blame upon me.	Si ha perdido su dinero, no debe echar la culpa á mí.
You had not seen him when he wrote to me.	V. no le habia visto, cuando me escribió.
What have you to say to me?	Que tiene V. que decirme?
I complimented him on the occasion.	Le dí la enhorabuena, segun pedia la ocasion.

Nobody understood mankind better than La Bruyere.	Nadie conocia mejor á los hombres que La Bruyere.
There is nothing to be seen.	No hay nada que ver
You will find them at my uncle's.	V. los encontrará en casa de mi tio.
Take care to do what I told you.	Cuidado que haga V. lo que le he dicho.
In less than three weeks we shall begin harvest,	En ménos de tres semanas empezarémos la cosecha.
He is an enemy to ceremony.	Es enemigo de ceremonias.
They acted more prudently and more politely than I thought.	Se condujéron con mas prudencia y política de lo que yo habia creido
Do not maintain so absurd an opinion.	No mantenga V. opinion tan absurda.
I do not lose all my time.	No pierdo todo mi tiempo
He loves nothing, he cares for nothing.	No quiere á nada, de nada le da cuidado.
How I pity the poor girl!	¡Que lástima me da la pobre muchacha!
What a deal of trouble papa gives himself for us!	¡Cuanta pena se toma papá por nosotros!
He succours the unfortunate, because he pities them.	Ayuda á los desdichados porque tiene lástima de ellos.
It is very hard to have neither money nor friends.	Es muy duro el no tener ni dinero ni amigos.
Is not his brother a merchant?	Su hermano no es comerciante?

No, he is a physician.	No, es médico.
These shoes are too narrow, they hurt me.	Estos zapatos estan demasiado estrechos, me lastiman.
I must always repeat the same thing to you.	Tengo que repetirle á V siempre la misma cosa.
This is precisely what I intended to do with it.	Es precisamente lo que queria hacer con ello.
Have you forgotten me already?	Me ha olvidado V. ya?
Do you not expect to be soon master of that business?	No espera V. pronto conocer perfectamente su oficio?
I am going there this instant, and you may depend upon my bringing it.	Voy allá al instante, y V. puede depender que lo traeré conmigo.
He is a dangerous man; I will have nothing to do with him.	Es hombre peligroso; no quiero negocio con él.
I am no judge of painting.	No conozco bien la pintura.
Let us bury the past in oblivion, and let us now live good friends.	Olvidémos lo pasado, y seámos buenos amigos.
How unfortunate he is to have married a woman of that kind!	¡Que desgraciado es en haberse casado con mujer de esa clase!
We have been long in expectation of his return.	Hace mucho tiempo que estamos esperando que vuelva.
Have you read any novels?	Ha leido V. algunas novelas?
I am reading one now.	Estoy leyendo una ahora

Your father enjoys good health, yet he is above seventy.	Su padre de V. goza de buena salud, á pesar de tener mas de setenta años.
I am certain he will sell you his estate.	Estoy seguro que le venderá á V. su propiedad.
Shall we have any letters to-day?	Tendrémos cartas hoy?
I do not well understand that.	No entiendo bien eso.
If it were so, somebody would have mentioned it.	Si fuera así, alguno lo hubiera dicho.
I neither play nor dance.	Ni toco ni bailo.
What have you been saying to him to put him into such a passion?	Que le ha dicho V. para ponerle tan lleno de cólera?
I had suspected that you would be the loser by it.	Habia sospechado que V perderia en eso.
Prevent him from doing mischief.	Impídale de hacer daño.
I do not like it, and you will oblige me by speaking no more about it.	No me gusta, y me hará V un favor en no hablar mas de eso.
I see you do not complain without cause.	Veo que V. no se queja sin razon.
It is ten to one that he cannot perform what he has promised.	Se puede apostar diez contra uno, que no hará lo que ha prometido.
A more rainy or cold season was never known.	Tiempo mas lluvioso y frio nunca se ha conocido.
You must be very foolish.	V. debe ser muy bobo

Don't do it, unless I give you leave.	No haga V. eso sin permiso.
He is a merchant, of whose honour and probity there can be no doubt.	Es un comerciante, de cuya honradez y probidad no se puede dudar.
How many children has he?	Cuantos niños tiene?
I told you he had but one.	Le dije á V. que no tenia mas que uno.
You may go and take a walk in the garden, but do not touch anything whatever.	Puedes ir á pasearte en la huerta, pero no toques nada.
Your cousin wishes to walk with us, but we do not want his company.	Su primo quiere pasearse con nosotros, pero no necesitamos de su compañia.
When did you hear from your sister?	Cuando recibió V. carta de su hermana?
We heard from her since her departure.	Recibímos noticias suyas despues que se marchó.
What! must I set out without speaking to him?	¡Que! ¿tengo que marcharme sin decirle nada?
He related it to many persons, but no one would believe him.	Lo dijo á mucha gente, pero nadie lo quiso creer.
She lost her voice by singing too late in the garden.	Perdió la voz por haber cantado demasiado tarde en el jardin.
Look at that little tree near you; it is loaded with blossoms.	Mire ese arbolito cerca de V.; está cargado de flores.
Why don't you do that?	Porqué no hace V. eso?

22

He has spent all the money his father sent him.	Ha gastado todo el dinero que le mandó su padre.
Figure to yourself the doctor in the middle of a ball-room.	Figúrese V. al médico en medio del baile.
Stop a little if you please, you are to go after me.	Hágame el favor de esperarse un poco, pues debe V. ir detras de mí.
Our general lost his left arm in the battle.	Nuestro general perdió el brazo izquierdo en la batalla.
What! are you not gone yet?	¡Que! ¿no se marchó V. todavía?
I see by your discourse that you are acquainted with this business.	Veo por su discurso que V. conoce bien este negocio.
Hear me to the end, without interrupting me.	Escúcheme hasta el fin, sin interrumpirme.
This child has a pretty little mouth.	Esta niña tiene una boquita muy bonita.
It is full a mile from our house to the church.	Hay una buena milla de nuestra casa á la iglésia.
The lady who dined with us, is the same you saw ten years ago at Boston.	La Señora que comió en casa, es la misma que V. vió hace diez años en Boston.
Children seldom forget, when they exert themselves and study attentively.	Los niños rara vez olvidan, cuando se esfuerzan y estudian atentamente.
Will they go to the concert this evening?	Iran al concierto esta noche?
He dares not to contradict me	No se atreve á contradecirme

I know the means by which he gained this point.	Conozco los medios de que se valió para ganar este punto.
He speaks of I know not what.	Habla de no sé qué.
She lives near the market-place.	Vive cerca de la plaza
Ought we to judge of a work only by the impression it makes upon us?	Debemos juzgar de una obra solamente por la impresion que nos ha causado?
He returned our visits, but declines all society.	Nos ha pagado nuestras visitas, mas se exime de toda sociedad
He appears to be a man of retired habits.	Parece ser un hombre de costumbres retiradas
Relate to us the particulars of your journey.	Recítenos V. los incidentes de su viage.
They entered together into a commercial speculation.	Entráron juntos en una especulacion mercantil
To some people, dinner is one of the most momentous concerns of their lives.	Para algunos hombres, el comer es uno de los asuntos mas perentórios de su vida.
He had an able and elegant style of writing.	Tenia un erudito y elegante estilo de escribir
Dinner had just been announced when my cousin arrived; but we were still in the drawing-room.	Acabában de anunciar la comida cuando llegó mi primo; pero estábamos todavia en el salon de comer.
She covered her face to conceal her tears.	Se cubrió la cara para ocultar sus lágrimas.

I beg your pardon, I ought not to have made you wait so long.	Perdone V., no debia haberle hecho esperar tanto tiempo.
Let us go into those little walks.	Vámos por esas estrechas sendas.
I assure you there is a great deal of pleasure in teaching attentive scholars.	Le aseguro á V. que hay mucho gusto en enseñar á discípulos atentos.
This is merely an object of curiosity.	Es solamente un objeto de curiosidad.
This is the place where that man was killed.	Aquí está el punto en donde matáron á ese hombre.
The brewer and baker are gone, but the butcher and grocer are at the door.	Se marcháron el cervecero y el panadero, pero el carnicero y el especiero están á la puerta.
That man who walks along the meadow, had formerly a hundred thousand dollars; he is now obliged to work for his livelihood.	Ese hombre que está paseándose por el prado, tenia cien mil pesos; y ahora tiene que trabajar para ganar su vida.
The company which he keeps will destroy his reputation.	La compañía en que anda, destruirá su reputacion
Every time I see him, I take him for a foreigner.	Cada vez que le veo, me parece estrangero.
It is not so cold as it was at the beginning of this month.	No hace tanto frio como al principio del mes.
Go and put everything in order	Vete á poner todo en órden.

It is no more than six months since he bought a house for a thousand dollars.	No hace mas de seis meses que compró una casa por mil pesos.
Two days after he sold it for two thousand five hundred.	Dos dias despues lo vendió por dos mil quinientos.
It is to continual study that your brother owes his great learning.	Su hermano debe su gran saber al continuo estúdio.
She spends all her time in reading novels.	Pasa todo su tiempo en leer novelas.
How shall we spend our time?	Como pasarémos el tiempo?
We have been studying latin these eight years.	Hace ocho años que estamos estudiando el latin.
We shall seize the first opportunity to thank him for his kindness.	Nos aprovecharémos la primera ocasion para darle las gracias por su bondad.
How long will it be before you send me what I have just spoken of?	Cuanto tiempo se pasará ántes que V. me mande de lo que acabo de hablarle?
It does not become a young lady to ramble about in this manner.	No se mira bien que una Señorita ande por ahí vagando de ese modo.
This fault must be excused in consideration of his youth.	Se debe perdonar ese error en consideracion a su juventud.
He is an amiable man who has done that.	Es hombre amable él que ha hecho eso.
I want to get rid of that man.	Quiero desembarazarme de ese hombre.

My attachment for you made me overlook many things.	El cariño que le tenia á V. me ha hecho descuidar muchas cosas.
Come. we shall play a game at chess, and then talk.	Vámos, juguemos una partida de axedrez, y despues hablarémos.
She told me you were in the secret.	Me dijo que V. estaba en el secreto.
I saw four fine horses in his stable.	Ví cuatro hermosos caballos en su cuadra.
It was too dear by half.	Era mas de la mitad de lo que valia.
The ladies after whom you inquire, are gone to France.	Las Señoras por quienes está V. preguntando, se fuéron á Francia.
Why do you follow me as you do?	Porqué me sigue V. de este modo?
I am going to prepare everything I want for my journey.	Voy á preparar todo lo que necesito para mi viage.
She is not inclined to pay that attention to her studies which her sister does, consequently her improvement is less.	No está dispuesta á atender á sus estudios como su hermana, de suerte que adelanta ménos.
I wish we had invited that gentleman to dinner: I think him an amiable and sensible man; his conservation pleased me extremely.	Me hubiera gustado mucho que V. convidase á comer á ese Señor: me parece amable y hombre de talento; me gustó mucho su conversacion.
If you do not succeed, it will not be my fault.	Si V. no sale bien, no es culpa mia.

He did it, I know not how.	Lo hizo, no sé como.
I ride on horseback every day.	Monto á caballo todos los dias.
Go and fetch me some ink.	Vaya á buscarme tinta.
Stay, is there none in that bottle yonder?	Espere, ¿no hay allá en aquella botella?
He complains of I know not what?	Se queja de no sé qué.
There will be a great deal of company at our house to-night.	Habrá mucha gente en casa esta noche.
We waited for them a month.	Los esperámos un mes.
It is at least a twelvemonth since I saw her.	Hay á lo ménos un año que no la he visto.
Go near the fire, you are wet.	Acérquese al fuego; está V. mojado.
When shall we have French beans?	Cuando tendrémos avas de Fráncia?
They are not in blossom yet.	Todavia no estan en flor.
There is a real advantage in being learned, but science must not create pride.	Hay mucha ventaja en ser docto, pero la ciencia no debe engendrar el orgullo.
Should he not arrive, I should go there.	Si no viniera, iria yo allá.
I will try to render myself worthy of the friendship with which you honour me.	Trataré de hacerme digno de la amistad con que V. me honra.
He noticed that he was not so cordially received as usual.	Advirtió que no fué tan bien recibido como de costumbre.

We learn French, and understand very well all that is said to us in that language.	Aprendemos el Frances y entendemos perfectamente todo lo que se nos dice en aquella lengua.
I shall not go shooting any more this season.	No iré mas á la caza este año.
You must get up to-morrow at four o'clock.	V, tendrá que levantarse mañana á las cuatro.
How do you spend your time?	Como pasa V. el tiempo?
If it is not an indiscretion on my part, pray tell me what passed between you and them.	Si no es una indiscrecion de mi parte, hágame el favor de decirme lo que se pasó entre V. y ellos.
How long has he been dead?	Cuanto hace que murió?
He died four years ago.	Murió hace cuatro años.
Bring the tea-pot and the tea things.	Traiga V. la tetera y el servicio de té.
Here they are with the cups.	Aquí estan con las tazas.
Have you not interrupted me several times?	No me ha interrumpido V. muchas veces?
I like these sentences, because they are short and instructive.	Me gustan estas frases, porque son cortas é instructivas.
I met him running as fast as he could.	Le encontré corriendo cuanto podia.
What is that to me? No more of that, I beg of you.	Que me importa eso? Acaba con eso, por Dios.
What did you do on Tuesday last?	Que hizo V el Mártes pasado?

As he works hard in the day-time, it is no wonder he should be sleepy at night.	Como trabaja mucho de dia, no es milagro que tenga sueño de noche.
As I do not understand politics, I never meddle with it; and so, I have no news to tell you.	Como no entiendo de política, nunca me mezclo en ella; así no tengo noticias que darle á V.
I hope we shall spend many happy hours together in the holidays.	Espero que pasarémos juntos muchas horas felices, durante las vacaciones.
I have not read the book; I only looked through it.	No he leido el libro; lo he mirado solamente
I took but little part in the conversation at table; but I was much pleased with the propriety and good humour of the party.	Apénas he tomado parte en la conversacion de la mesa; mas estaba muy divertido por la decencia y buen humor que reinaba entre la compañia.
I must own I am best pleased with whatever requires the least time and preparation.	Confieso que me gusta mas lo que requiere ménos tiempo y ménos preparacion.
After having waited for her a long time, she sent me word that she was not ready to go out.	Despues de haberle esperado mucho tiempo, me mandó decir que no estaba lista para salir.
You sing better than you did.	V. canta mucho mejor que hace poco.
I shall go and see her after dinner	Iré á verla despues de comer.

I have spent many happy moments here.	Aquí he pasado algunos ratos muy felices.
They intend to visit Rome, and then to go to Naples.	Tienen intencion de ir á Roma, y de allí á Nápoles.
What book do you translate?	Que libro está V. traduciendo?
I was near falling from my horse	Me faltó poco para caer de mi caballo.
She cannot open her mouth but she says some foolish thing or other.	No puede abrir la boca sin decir algun disparate.
I know none of the merchants of this place.	No conozco á ningun comerciante de este pueblo.
Sister, who gave you this letter?	Hermana, ¿quien te dió esta carta?
Miss D.'s servant.	La criada de la Señorita D.
I have not seen you these six weeks.	No le he visto á V. hace seis semanas.
Should we set out this afternoon, we shall let you know.	Si nos marchamos esta tarde, le mandarémos avisar á V.
Write to me by the first post, that I may receive your letter before my departure for California.	Escríbeme por el primer correo, de modo que yo pueda recibir su carta ántes de marcharme para la California.
California.	La California.
Are you going to California?	Va V á la California?
Well, I havn't quite made up my mind.	No me he decidido todavia.

DETACHED SENTENCES.

There are a great many gone from New York.	Se han ido muchos de Nueva York.
Yes, and from all parts of the United States.	Si, y de todas partes de los Estados Unidos.
I sail to-morrow.	Mañana nos hacemos á la vela.
In what ship?	En que barco?
Do you cross the Isthmus?	Pasa V. por el Istmo?
No, I prefer going round the Horn.	No, prefiero ir por el Cabo de Hornos.
I am going over-land from Vera Cruz.	Voy por tierra, desde Vera-Cruz.
I don't like that route.	No me gusta ese camino.
Are you a member of any company?	¿Es V. miembro de alguna compañia?
No, Sir, I am going out with merchandise on my own account.	No, Señor, voy con mercancias de mi cuenta.
Do you take any segars?	Toma V. algunos tabacos?
A few thousands for my own use.	Algunos millares para mi uso.
They will fetch a high price there.	Deben venderse á buen precio allá.
A good Havana will sell for a pinch of gold dust.	Un buen tabaco de la Havana se venderá por una pulgarada de oro en polvo.
What is gold dust selling at an ounce?	A como se vende la onza de oro en polvo?
At all prices	A todos precios.
How is that?	Como es eso?
Provisions are so scarce, that the diggers are obliged to sacrifice al-	Los víveres estan tan escasos, que los cavadores se ven obligados á sa-

most all their gold to keep life and soul together.	crificar casi todo su oro para mantenerse.
Have you bought a washing machine?	Ha comprado V. máquina para lavar?
Do you want to buy any sieves?	Quiere V. comprar cedazos?
Are you well armed?	Está V. bien armado?
Will you trade gold for segars?	Quiere V. cambiar oro por tabacos?
How much do you ask for that brace of pistols?	Cuanto pide V. por ese par de pistolas?
They say it is easier to pick up than to keep gold in California.	Dicen que en California es mas fácil cojer el oro que guardarlo.
So it is in all countries.	Así es en todos los paises.
In a few months, goods will be as cheap in California as in New York.	En pocos meses, los géneros estaran tan baratos en California como en Nueva York.
Some kind of government must be established immediately.	Es necesario establecer alguna clase de gobierno, inmediatamente.
What a fine breeze!	¡Que brisa tan hermosa!
We are out at sea.	Estamos en alta mar.
Where do we put in for provisions?	Adonde arribamos para tomar víveres?
Have you any grog on board?	Tiene V. licor abordo?
I never drink spirits.	Nunca bebo licores.
Won't you take something with me?	No quiere V. tomar algo conmigo?
I will take a little Soda water.	Tomaré un poco de Soda.

My berth is wet.	Mi camarote está mojado.
The captain is a first-rate fellow.	El capitan es muy buen muchacho.
We are rather short of provisions.	Estamos un poco escasos de provisiones.
Who is at the helm?	Quien va al timon?
There is a man fallen overboard.	Ha caido un hombre á la mar.
Lower the boat.	Baje el bote.
A shark has swallowed him.	Le ha tragado un tiburon.
Poor fellow!	¡El pobre!
Do you see that ship?	Ve V. ese buque?
It is a British bark.	Es una barca inglesa.
It is an American schooner.	Es una goleta americana.
It is a Spanish ship.	Es un buque español.
It is a Portuguese brig.	Es un bergantin portugues.
A sloop-of-war.	Una corveta de guerra.
The steamship Crescent City.	El buque de vapor Crescent City.
We are getting short of water.	Nos va escaseando el agua.
Will our provisions hold out?	Tendrémos bastantes víveres?
You must keep friends with the steward and cook.	Es preciso hacerse amigos del dispensero y del cocinero.
Are you going ashore?	Va V. á tierra?
Let's smoke a segar.	Fumémos un tabaco.
When does the vessel sail?	Cuando sale el buque?
How many passengers has she?	Cuantos pasageros tiene?
Have you engaged your passage?	Ha tomado V. su pasage?

I can't go yet.	Todavia no puedo ir.
Don't gamble.	No juegue V.
You will lose your money and your reputation too.	Perderá V. su dinero y su reputacion tambien.
We take in water and provisions at Rio Janeiro.	Tomamos agua y víveres en Rio Janeiro.
I want a good stock of segars for California.	Quiero un buen lote de tabacos para la California.
What kind do you want?	Que clase quiere V.?
Havana segars.	Tabacos de la Havana.
Where can I get the best?	En donde podré hallar los mejores?
At the "Havana Segar Mart."	En el "Havana Segar Mart."
Where is that?	En donde está eso?
In Water street.	En la calle de Water.
What number?	Que número?
Number 205.	Número dos cientos cinco.
At the corner of Fulton and Water streets.	En la esquina de Fulton y Water.
At Mr. Butler's.	En casa del Sr. de Butler.
O yes, I have heard of him.	Es verdad, he oido hablar de él.
He taught me to speak Spanish	Me enseñó hablar Español.
He sells nothing but the pure Havana.	No vende sino puros Havanos.
He is doing a large business.	Está haciendo buenos negocios.
He warrants all he sells.	Garantiza todo lo que vende.

He has written a little work on the Spanish language.	Ha escrito una obrita de la lengua Española.
You can't get a bad segar from his establishment.	No puede V. hallar mal tabaco en su establecimiento.
I'll give him a call tomorrow.	Pasaré á verle mañana.
He has Havana segars at all prices, from fourteen to fifty dollars a thousand.	Tiene tabacos de la Habana á todos precios, de catorce á cincuenta pesos el millar.
Does he sell many?	Vende muchos?
Yes, a great many.	Sí, muchísimos.
Buy of him once, and you will be sure to call again.	Compre V. de él una vez, y no dejará V. de volver.
As he keeps no domestic segars, you cannot be deceived.	Como no tiene tabacos del pais, no puede V. ser engañado.
Does he keep all kinds?	Tiene de todas clases?
O yes: Regalias, Panetelas, Caballeros, Cañones. Damas, London size, pressed segars; in fine, a large variety of the choicest brands, and all warranted genuine	Sí: Regalias, Panetelas, Caballeros, Cañones, Damas, Lóndres, tabacos prensados; en fin, una variedad muy grande de las mejores marcas, y todos garantizados.

VERBS.*

There are six kinds of verbs, viz.: ACTIVE PASSIVE, NEUTER, REFLECTED, RECIPROCAL, and IMPERSONAL.

Active, when the object is direct. Example: *Como* patatas; I eat potatoes.

Passive, formed from the Active, taking the direct object for its subject. Ex.: Las patatas son *comidas;* the potatoes are eaten.

Neuter, when the verb can admit of no object. Ex.: *Soy*, I am; *duermo*, I sleep.

Reflected, when the subject and the object are the same person. Ex.: *Se* mató; he killed himself.

Reciprocal, expressing several subjects acting on each other. Ex.: Los buenos amigos deben amarse; good friends ought to love each other.

Impersonal, when only used in the third person singular. Ex.: *Llueve*, it rains; *tronaba*, it was thundering.

Conjugation of the verbs ESTAR *and* SER, To Be, *omitting compound tenses, which may be formed by the student.*

Infinitive.

Estar, ser, To be.
Estando, siendo, Being.
Estado, sido, Been.

---

* The conjugation of any verb may be found immediately by the following rule; if not in the list of Irregular Verbs, it must be conjugated regular, according to its termination; if ending in *ar*, first conjugation, *er* second, *ir* third.

Indicative Present

Estoy, soy, I am.
Estás, eres, Thou art.
Está, es, He is.
Estamos, somos, We are.
Estais, sois, You are.
Están, son, They are

Imperfect.

Estaba, era, I was.
Estabas, eras, Thou wast.
Estaba, era, He was.
Estábamos, éramos, We were
Estábais, érais, You were.
Estaban, eran, They were.

Perfect.

Estube, fuí, I was.
Estubiste, fuiste, Thou wast.
Estubo, fué, He was.
Estubímos, fuímos, We were.
Estubísteis, fuísteis, You were
Estubiéron, fuéron, They were.

Future.

Estaré, seré, I shall or will be.
Estarás, serás, Thou shalt or wilt be.
Estará, será, He shall or will be.
Estarémos, serémos, We shall or will be
Estaréis, seréis, You shall or will be.
Estarán, serán, They shall or will be.

Conditional.

Estaria, seria, I should or would be.
Estarias, serias, Thou shouldst or wouldst be
Estaria, seria, He should or would be.
Estaríamos, seríamos, We should or would be.
Estaríais, seríais, You should or would be.
Estarian, serian, They should or would be

Imperative.

Está tú, sé tú, Be thou.
Esté él, sea él, Be he.
Estad vosotros, sed vosotros, Be you.
Esten ellos, sean ellos, Be they.

Subjunctive Present.

Esté, sea, I may be.
Estes, seas, Thou mayest be.
Esté, sea, He may be.
Estemos, seamos, We may be.
Esteis, seais, You may be
Esten, sean, They may be.

Imperfect.

Fuera, fuese, estubiera, estubiese, I might be.
Fueras fueses, estubieras, estubieses, Thou mightest be.
Fuera, fuese, estubiera, estubiese, He might be.
Fuéramos, fuésemos, estubiéramos, estubiésemos, We might be.
Fuérais, fuéseis, estubiérais, estubiéseis, You might be.
Fuéran, fuesen, estubieran, estubiesen, They might be.

Ser and Estar.

These verbs both being expressed in English by the verb To be, require some explanation. Estar, alone is used when it implies being in any place. Estar is used to signify a passing state, or temporary condition of person or thing. Ex. of place :—Estoy aquí, I am here; Estaba en casa, I was at home. You cannot say : Soy aquí ; era en casa. Ex. of a passing state or temporary condition ;—Estoy cojo, I am lame (meaning not a fixed lameness) ; Estoy enfadado, I am angry ; Está enamorado, He is in love. When you wish to express an inherent quality of mind or body, or a natural state of things, use Ser. Ex. :—Esa Señorita es muy bonita, That young lady is very pretty ; La virtud es amable, Virtue is amiable ; Es cojo, He is lame (meaning a lame man, always lame). Ese muchacho está muy sucio, That boy is very dirty (meaning now, and not naturally so) ; Ese muchacho es muy sucio, That boy is very dirty (or a dirty boy, inclined to be dirty). Es pais muy frio, It is a very cold country ; La sopa está fria, The soup is cold ; El perro está rabioso, The dog is mad ; Los huevos son buenos, Eggs are good ; Los huevos son blancos, Eggs are white.

Without further remarks, I leave the learner to the exercise of his own judgment, founded on the few examples here given.

HABER and TENER, To Have

Infinitive.

Haber, tener, To Have.
Habiendo, teniendo, Having.
Hábido, tenido, Had.

Indicative Present.

He, tengo, I have.
Has, tienes, Thou hast.
Ha, tiene, He has.
Hemos, tenemos, We have
Habeis, teneis, You have.
Han, tienen, They have.

Imperfect.

Habia, tenia, I had.
Habias, tenias, Thou hadst.
Habia, tenia, He had.
Habíamos, teníamos, We had
Habíais, teníais, You had.
Habian, tenian, They had.

Perfect.

Hube, tuve, I had.
Hubiste, tuviste, Thou hadst.
Hubo, tuvo, He had.
Hubímos, tuvímos, We had.
Hubísteis, tuvísteis, You had.
Hubiéron, tuviéron, They had

Future.

Habré, tendré, I shall or will have.
Habrás, tendrás, Thou shalt have.
Habrá, tendrá, He will have.
Habrémos, tendrémos, We shall have.
Habréis, tendréis, You will have
Habrán, tendrán, They shall have

Conditional.

Habria, tendria, I should or would have.
Habrias, tendrias, Thou wouldst have.
Habria, tendria, He would have.
Habríamos, tendríamos, We would have.
Habríais, tendríais, You would have.
Habrian, tendrian, They would have.

Imperative.

Ten tú, Have thou.
Tenga él, Let him have.
Tengámos nosotros, Let us have.
Tened vosotros, Have you.
Tengan ellos, Let them have.

Subjunctive Present.

Que haya, tenga, That I may have.
Hayas, tengas, Thou mayest have.
Haya, tenga, He may have.
Hayamos, tengamos, We may have.
Hayais, tengais, You may have.
Hayan, tengan, They may have.

Imperfect.

Que hubiera, hubiese, tubiera, tubiese, That I might have.
Hubieras, hubieses, tubieras, tubieses, Thou mightest have.
Hubiera, hubiese, tubiera, tubiese, He might have.
Hubiéramos, hubiésemos, tubiéramos, tubiésemos. We might have.
Hubiérais, hubiéseis, tubiérais, tubiéseis, You might have.
Hubieran, hubiesen, tubieran, tubiesen, They might have.

Haber and Tener.

Haber is used simply as an auxiliary, and never to signify possession. Ex.:—He visto, I have seen; El ha comido, He has dined, &c.

Tener is used to signify the absolute possession of any thing, as: Tengo padre, I have a father; Tendrá dinero, He will have money.

It is very important to commit to memory the auxiliary verbs, as without them the rest are of little service.

Haber is also used impersonally: *Hay*, there is, there are; Habia, there was, there were, &c.

There are three conjugations in Spanish, the first ending in *ar*, the second in *er*, the third in *ir*.*

FIRST CONJUGATION.

AMAR, To Love.

Infinitive.

Amar, To love.   Amando, Loving.   Amado, Loved

Indicative Present.

Amo, I love.   Amamos, We love.
Amas, Thou lovest.   Amais, You love.
Ama, He loves.   Aman, They love

Imperfect.

Amaba, I loved or was loving.
Amabas, Thou lovedst.
Amaba, He loved.
Amabamos, We loved.
Amábais, You loved.
Amában, They loved.

Perfect.

Amé, I loved.   Amámos, We loved.
Amaste, Thou lovedst.   Amásteis, You loved
Amó, He loved.   Amáron, They loved.

---

* Verbs undergoing the same changes as either of these three are termed regular.

Future.

Amaré, I shall or will love.
Amarás, Thou wilt love.
Amará, He will love.
Amarémos, We will love.
Amaréis, You will love.
Amarán, They will love

Conditional.

Amaria, I should or would love.
Amarias, Thou wouldst love.
Amaria, He would love.
Amaríamos, We would love.
Amaríais, You would love.
Amarian, They would love.

Imperative.

Ama, Love thou.
Ame, Let him love.
Amémos, Let us love
Amad, Love ye.
Amen, Let them love.

Subjunctive Present.

Que ame, That I may love
Ames, Thou mayest love.
Amè, He may love.
Amemos, we may love.
Ameis, You may love.
Amen, They may love.

Imperfect.

Que amara, amase, That I might love
Amaras, amáses, Thou mightest love.
Amara, amase, He might love.
Amáramos, amásemos, We might love.
Amárais, amáseis, You might love.
Amaran, amasen, They might love.

IRREGULAR VERBS OF THE FIRST CONJUGATION.

The following verbs are conjugated like AMAR, with these exceptions:

Indicative Present.—Acierto, aciertas, acierta acertamos, acertais, aciertan.

Imperative.—Acierta, acierto, acertad, acierten.

Subjunctive Present.—Acierte, aciertes, acierte acertemos, acerteis, acierten.

Acertar.	Aventarse.	Desatentar.
Acrecentar.	Calentar.	Desatravesar.
Adestrar.	Cegar.	Decimentar.
Alentar.	Cerrar.	Desconcertar.
Apacentar.	Cimentar.	Desempedrar.
Arrendar.	Comenzar.	Desencerrar.
Asentar.	Concertar.	Desenterrar.
Aserrar.	Confesar.	Deshelar.
Asestar.	Denegar.	Desherrar.
Atentar.	Derrengar.	Desmembrar.
Aterrar.	Desacertar.	Despedrar.
Atestar.	Desalentar.	Despernar.
Atravesar.	Desapretar.	Despertar.
Aventar.	Desasosegar.	Desplegar.

Desterrar.
Diezmar.
Empedrar.
Empezar.
Encerrar.
Encomendar.
Enmendar.
Ensangrentar.
Enterrar.
Errar.
Escalentar.
Escarmentar.
Estregar.
Fregar.
Gobernar.
Helar.

Herrar.
Incensar.
Invernar.
Manifestar.
Mentar.
Merendar.
Negar.
Nevar.
Pensar.
Plegar.
Quebrar.
Recomendar.
Regar.
Remendar.
Renegar.

Requebrar.
Retemblar.
Retentar.
Reventar.
Segar.
Sembrar.
Sentarse.
Serrar.
Sosegar.
Sosegarse.
Soterrar.
Temblar.
Tentar.
Trasegar.
Tropezar.

The following are conjugated like AMAR, with these exceptions:

Indicative Present.—Acuerdo, acuerdas, acuerda; acuerdan.

Imperative.—Acuerda, acuerde, acordad, acuerden.

Subjunctive Present.—Acuerde, acuerdes, acuerde acordemos, acordeis, acuerden.

Acordar.
Acordarse.
Acordar á uno.
Acostarse.
Augurar.
Almorzar.
Amolar.
Aportar.

Apostar.
Aprobar.
Asolar.
Asoldar.
Asonar.
Atronar.
Avergonzar.
Avergonzarse.

Colar.
Colgar.
Comprobar.
Contar.
Concordar.
Costar.
Consolar.
Degollar

VERBS.

Demostrar.	Encordar.	Resonar
Denostar.	Engrosar	Revelar.
Desacordar.	Enrodar.	Revolcarse
Desaprobar.	Esforzar.	Rodar.
Descolgar.	Forzar.	Rogar.
Descollar.	Holgar.	Soldar.
Desconsolar.	Hollar.	Soltar.
Descontar.	Jugar.	Sonar.
Desengrosar.	Mostrar.	Sonarse.
Desflocar.	Poblar.	Soñar.
Desfogarse.	Probar	Tostar.
Desollar.	Recordar.	Trascolar.
Desovar.	Recordarse.	Trascordarse
Despoplar.	Recostarse.	Trasoñar
Destronar.	Refortar.	Trocar.
Desvergonzarse.	Renovar.	Tronar.
Emporcar.	Reprobar.	Volar,
Encontrar.	Resollar.	Volcar.

Andar ; exceptions as follows :

Ind. Perfect.—Anduve, anduviste, anduvo, anduvimos, anduvísteis, anduviéron.

Subj. Imperfect.—Anduviera, anduviese, &c.

Dar ; exceptions :

Ind Present.—Doy, I give, &c.
Perfect.—Dí, diste, dió, dímos, dísteis, **diéron**
Subj. Imperfect.—Diera, diese, &c.

SECOND CONJUGATION.

TEMER, To Fear.

Infinitive.

Present. Temer, To fear.
Gerund. Temiendo, Fearing.
Past Part. Temido, Feared.

Indicative Present.

Temo, I fear. Tememos, We fear.
Temes, Thou fearest. Temeis, You fear.
Teme, He fears. Temen, They fear.

Imperfect.

Temia, I feared or was fearing.
Temias, Thou fearedst,
Temia, He feared.
Temíamos, We feared.
Temíais You feared.
Temian, They feared

Perfect.

Temí, I feared.
Temiste, Thou fearedst.
Temió, He feared.
Temímos, We feared.
Temísteis, You feared.
Temiéron, They feared.

Future.

Temeré, I shall or will fear.
Temerás, Thou wilt fear.
Temerá, He will fear.
Temerémos, We will fear.
Temeréis, You will fear.
Temerán, they will fear.

Conditional.

Temeria, I should or would fear.
Temerias, thou shouldst fear.
Temeria, He would fear.
Temeríamos, we should fear.
Temeríais, you would fear.
Temerian, They should fear

Imperative

Teme, Fear thou.
Tema, Let him fear.
Temámos, Let us fear.
Temed, Fear you.
Teman, Let them fear.

Subjunctive Present.

Que tema, That I may fear.
Temas, Thou mayest fear.
Tema, He may fear
Temamos, We may fear.
Temais, You may fear.
Teman, They may fear.

VERBS 283

Imperfect.

Que temiera, temiese, That I might fear.
Temieras, temieses, Thou mightest fear.
Temiera, temiese, He might fear.
Temiéramos, temiésemos, We might fear.
Temiéreis, temiéseis, You might fear.
Temieren, temiesen, They might fear.

IRREGULAR VERBS OF THE SECOND CONJUGATION.

The following verbs are conjugated like TEMER with these exceptions:
Indicative Present.—Aborrezco, I abhor.
Imperative.—Aborrezca, aborrezcan.
Subj. Present.—Aborrezca, &c.

Aborrecer.
Acaecer.
Adolecer.
Adormecer.
Agradecer.
Amanecer.
Amortecerse.
Anochecer.
Aparecer.
Apetecer.
Aterecer.
Carecer.
Compadecerse.
Complacer.
Conocer.
Convalecer.

Crecer.
Desabastecer.
Desadormecer.
Desaparecer.
Desconocer.
Desentorpecer.
Desfallecer.
Desflaquecer.
Desguarnecer
Desobedecer.
Desvanecerse.
Embravecerse.
Embrutecerse.
Empobrecer.
Encallecer.
Encanecer

Encarecer.
Encrudecerse.
Encruelecer.
Endentecer.
Endurecer.
Enflaquecer.
Enfurecerse.
Engrandecer.
Enloquecer.
Enmohecerse.
Enmudecer.
Ennegrecer.
Ennoblecer.
Enrarecer.
Enriquecer.
Ensoberbecerse

Enternecer.	Favorecer.	Parecer.
Entumecer.	Fenecer.	Parecerse
Entontecerse	Fortalecer.	Perecer.
Entorpecerse.	Guarnecer.	Pertenecer
Entristecer.	Humedecer.	Prevalecer.
Entumecerse.	Merecer.	Reconocer.
Envejecer.	Nacer.	Reflorecer.
Escarnecer.	Obedecer.	Remanecer
Esclarecer.	Oscurecer.	Renacer.
Establecer.	Ofrecer.	Restablecer
Estremecerse.	Pacer.	Reverdecer.
Fallecer.	Padecer.	

The following are like TEMER, with these exceptions:

Ind. Present.—Atiendo, atiéndes, atiende, atendemos, atendeis, atienden.

Imperative.—Entiende, entienda, entended, entiendan.

Subj. Present.—Entienda, entiendas, entienda, entendamos, entendais, entiendan.

Atender.	Descender.	Heder.
Cerner.	Desentenderse.	Hender.
Condescender.	Encender.	Perder.
Contender.	Entender.	Reverter.
Defender.	Estender.	Trascender.
Desatender		

The following verbs are conjugated like TEMER, with these exceptions:

Absolver. *Past Participle.*—Absuelto.

Ind. Present.—Absuelvo, absuelves, absuelve, absolvemos, absolveis, absuelven.

Imperative.—Absuelve, absuelva, absolved, absuélvan

Subj. Present.—Absuelva, absuelvas, absuelva, absolvamos, absolvais, absuelvan.

Absolver.	Dolerse.	Remorder.
Condoler.	Envolver.	Remover.
Conmover.	Llover.	Resolver.
Desenvolver.	Moler.	Revolver.
Devolver.	Morder.	Solver.
Disolver.	Mover.	Vo ver.
Doler.	Promover.	Volverse.

Soler, only used in Present and Imperf. Ind.

Traer, and verbs ending in traer, are conjugated like Temer, with these exceptions:
Pres. Participle, Trayendo. Indic. Pres., Traigo, I carry. Perfect, Traje, trajiste, trajo, trajimos, trajísteis, trajéron. Imperative, Trae, traiga, traed, traigan. Subj. Pres., Traiga, &c. Imperfect, Trajera, trajese, &c.

Ver and compounds conjugated like Temer, with these exceptions:
Past Participle, Visto. Imperative, Ve, vea, veámos, ved, vean. Subj. Pres., Vea, veas, vea, veamos, veais, vean. Imperf., Viera, viese.

Tener and verbs derived from it; see Tener.

Hacer and its derivatives, have the following exceptions to Temer:
Ind. Pres., Hago. Imperfect, Hice, hiciste, hizo, hicímos, hicísteis, hiciéron. Future, Haré, &c. Cond., Haria, &c. Imperative, haz, haga, haced,

hagan. Sub. Pres., Haga, &c. Imp., Hiciera, hiciese.

Caber has the following irregularities :
Ind. Pres., Quepo. Perfect, Cupe, cupiste, cupo, cupímos, cupísteis, cupiéron. Future, Cabré, &c. No Imperative. Subj. Pres., Quepa, &c. Imperfect, cupiera, cupiese, &c.

Caer has the following exceptions :
Pres. Part., Cayendo. Ind. Pres., Caigo. Imperative, Cae, caiga, caed, caigan. Sub. Pres., Caiga, &c. Imp, Cayera, cayese.

Cocer, escocer, torcer, destorcer, descocer, have nearly the same exceptions as absolver, &c. Ind. Pres., Cuezco, cueces, cuece, cocemos, coceis, cuecen. Imperative, Cuece, cueza, coced, cuezan Sub. Pres., Cueza, cuézas, cueza, cozamos, cozais, cuezan.

Valer and equivaler: Ind. Pres., Valgo, I am worth. Future, Valdré, &c. Imperative, Vale, valga, valed, valgan. Sub. Pres., Valga, &c.

Haber : conjugated in full.—See Verbs.

Oler: Ind. Pres., Huelo, hueles, huele, olemos, oleis, huelen. Imperative, Huele, huela, oled, huelan. Subj. Pres., Huela, huelas, huela, olamos, olais, huelan.

Placer has only the following persons :
Ind. Present, Place, It pleases. Imp., Placia, It pleased. Perfect, Plugo, It pleased. Imperative. Plegue, Let it please. Subj. Pres., Plegue (á Dios), May it please God. Imp. Pluguiese.

Poder: Pres. Part., pudiendo. Ind. Pres., Puedo, puedes, puede, podemos, podeis, pueden. Perfect.

Pude, &c. Future, Podré, &c. No Imperative.
Sub. Pres., Pueda, puedas, pueda, podamos, podáis, puedan. Imperf., Pudiera, pudiese.

Querer: Ind. Pres., Quiero, quieres, quiere, queremos, quereis, quieren. Perfect, Quise, quisiste, quiso, quisímos, quisísteis, quisiéron. Fut., Querré, &c. Condit., Querria. Subj. Pres., Quiera, &c. Imperf., Quisiera, quisiese, &c.

Saber: Ind. Pres., Sé, I know. Perfect, Supe, supiste, supo, supímos, supísteis, supiéron. Future, Sabré, &c. Imperat., Sabe, sepa, sabed, sepan. Sub. Pres., Sepa, &a. Imp., Supiera, supiese, &c.

Poner and fourteen others ending in *poner*, are conjugated like Temer, with the following irregularities:
Past Part., Puesto. Indic. Present, Pongo, I put Perfect, Puse, pusiste, puso, pusimos, pusísteis, pusiéron. Future, Pondré, &c. Conditional, Pondria, &c. Subj. Pres., Ponga, &c. Imperfect, Pusiera, pusiese, &c. Imperative, Pon, ponga, pongámos, poned, pongan.

THIRD CONJUGATION.

SUFRIR, To Suffer.

Infinitive.

Present. Sufrir, To suffer.
Gerund. Sufriendo, Suffering
Past Part. Sufrido, Suffered

Indicative Present.

Sufro, I suffer.
Sufres, Thou sufferest,
Sufre, He suffers.
Sufrimos, We suffer.
Sufris, You suffer.
Sufren, They suffer

Imperfect.

Sufria, I suffered or was suffering
Sufrias, Thou sufferedst.
Sufria, He suffered.
Sufríamos, We suffered.
Sufríais, You suffered.
Sufrian, They suffered.

Perfect.

Sufrí, I suffered.
Sufriste, Thou sufferedst.
Sufrió, He suffered.
Sufrímos, We suffered.
Sufrísteis, You suffered.
Sufriéron, They suffered.

Future.

Sufriré, I shall or will suffer.
Sufrirás, Thou wilt suffer.
Sufrirá, He will suffer.
Sufrirémos, We shall suffer.
Sufriréis, You will suffer.
Sufrirán, They will suffer.

Conditional.

Sufriria, I should or would suffer.
Sufririas, Thou shouldst suffer
Sufriria, He should suffer.
Sufririamos, We should suffer.
Sufririais, You would suffer.
Sufririan, They would suffer

Imperative.

Sufre, Suffer thou.
Sufra, Let him suffer.
Sufrámos, Let us suffer
Sufrid, Suffer.
Sufran, Let them suffer.

Subjunctive Present.

Que sufra, That I may suffer
Sufras, Thou mayest suffer
Sufra, He may suffer.
Suframos, We may suffer.
Sufrais, You may suffer.
Sufran, They may suffer.

Imperfect

Que sufriera, sufriese, That I might suffer.
Sufrieras, sufrieses, Thou mightest suffer.
Sufriera, sufriese, He might suffer.
Sufriéramos, sufriésemos, We might suffer
Sufriérais, sufriéseis, You might suffer.
Sufrieran, sufriesen, They might suffer.

IRREGULAR VERBS OF THE THIRD CONJUGATION.

The following are conjugated like SUFRIR, except:

Ind. Present.—Adhiero, adhieres, adhiere, adherimos, adhereis, adhieren.

Perfect.—Adherí, adheriste, adhirió, adherimos adheristeis, adhirieron.

Imperative.—Adhiere, adhiera, adherid, adhieran.

Subj. Present.—Adhiera, adhieras, adhiera, adhiramos, adhirais, adhieran.

Adherir	Desmentir.	Mentir.
Advertir.	Diferir.	Pervertir.
Arrepentirse.	Digerir.	Preferir.
Asentir.	Divertir.	Presentir.
Conferir.	Herir.	Referir.
Consentir.	Hervir.	Requerir.
Controvertir	Inferir.	Resentirse.
Convertir.	Injerir.	Sentir.
Deferir.	Invertir.	

The following are like SUFRIR, with these exceptions:

Pres. Part.—Pidiendo. *Indic. Present.*—Pido, pides, pide, pedimos, pedis, piden.

Perfect.—Pidió, pidiéron.

Imperative.—Pide, pida, pidámos, pedid, pídan.

Subj. Pres.—Pida, &c.

Imp. Subj.—Pidiera, pidiese, &c.

Pedir.	Conducir.	Conseguir.
Apercibir.	Concebir.	Colegir.
Competir.	Ceñir	Constreñir.

VERBS.

Comedir.	Envestir.	Rendir.
Corregir.	Estreñir.	Reñir.
Comedirse.	Expedir.	Repetir.
Derretir.	Freir.	Reteñir.
Desceñir.	Gemir.	Revestir.
Descomedirse.	Impedir.	Seguir.
Desleir.	Investir.	Servir.
Despedir.	Medir.	Sonreir.
Desteñir.	Perseguir.	Teñir.
Despedirse.	Proseguir.	Vestir
Elegir.*	Regir.	Vestirse.
Engreirse.	Reir, or Reirse.	

Venir and its compounds, like Sufrir, with the following exceptions:
Pres. Part., Viniendo. Indicative Pres., Vengo. vienes, viene, venimos, venis, vienen. Perfect, Vine, veniste, vino, venimos, venistes, viniéron. Future, Vendré, &c. Imperat., Ven, venga, venid, vengan. Subj. Imperf., Viniera, viniese, &c.

Decir, Contradecir, Desdecir, have the following exceptions:
Past Part., Dicho. Ind. Pres., Digo. Perfect, Dije, dijiste, dijo, dijímos, dijísteis, dijéron. Imperative, Dí, diga, decid, digan. Subj. Pres., Diga, &c. Imperfect, Dijera, dijese.

Conducir, Deducir, Reducir, Introducir, Inducir, have the following exceptions:
Ind. Pres., Conduzco, I conduct. Perfect, Conduje, condujiste, condujo, condujímos, condujísteis, condujéron. Imperative, 3d. Pers. Sing, Conduzca;

---

* This verb changes g into j before a and o.

3d. Pers. Plur., Conduzcan. Subj. Pres., Conduzca, &c. Subj. Imp., Condujera, condujese, &c.

Lucir and its compounds have the same exceptions as Conducir, in the 1st. person Ind. Pres : in the Imperative, and in the Subj. Pres. The other parts are regular.

Cubrir, Descubrir, have the following exception Past Part., Cubierto

Dormir and Morir :
Pres. Part., Durmiendo. Ind. Pres., Duermo, duermes, duerme, dormimos, dormeis, duermen. Perf., Dormí, dormiste, durmió, dormimos, dormisteis, durmiéron. Imperat., Duerme, duerma, dormid, duérman. Subj. Pres., Duerma, duérmas, duerma, dormamos, durmais. duerman. Imperf., Durmiere, durmiese, &c.

Oir, Entreoir ͼ
Ind. Pres., Oigo, óyes, oye, oimos, ois, oyen. Perf., Oyó; oyéron. Imperat., Oye, oiga, oid, oigan. Subj. Present, Oiga, &c. Imperfect, Oyera, oyese, &c.

Erguir :
Part. Pres., Irguiendo. Ind. Pres., Yergo, yergues, yergue, erguimos, erguis, yerguen. Perfect, Irguió, irguiéron. Imperat., Yergue, yerga, erguid, yergan. Subj. Pres., Yerga, yergas, yerga, irgamos, irgais, yergan. Imperf., Erguiria, irguiera, &c.

Escribir and compounds. Past Part., Escrito.

Ir. Part. Pres., Yendo. Ind. Pres., Voy, vas, va, vamos, vais, van. Imperf., Iba, &c. Perfect, Fuí fuiste. fué. fuímos. fuísteis. fuéron. Impera

Ve, vaya, id, vayan. Subj. Pres., Vaya, &c. Imp., Fuero, fuese, &c.

Bendecir, Maldecir; exceptions to Decir, &c.:
Part. Past, Bendito Fut., Bendeciré, &c. Imperative, Bendice, bendiga, bendecid, bendigan.

Podrir. Past Part., Podrido. Conditional, third person, Podriria. Imperative, Podrid. Are all the parts used of this verb

Salir. Ind. Pres., Salgo, I go out. Fut., Saldré, &c. Imperative, Sal, salga, salid, salgan. Subj. Pres., Salgu, &c.

FIN.

www.ingramcontent.com/pod-product-compliance
Lightning Source LLC
Chambersburg PA
CBHW032056220426
43664CB00008B/1022